# feasting on raw foods

# feasting on raw foods

*edited by Charles Gerras*

**Featuring over 350 healthful no-cook recipes for every part of a meal—from appetizers through main course dishes to desserts**

**Special Contributions:**
Nancy Arobone, Ruth Cavin, Marilyn Cox, and Carol Meinhardt Hopkins

**Recipes:**
Readers of *Organic Gardening* ® Magazine
and Carole Collier
plus:
Linda Gilbert, Susan Hercek, Anita Hirsch, and Faye Martin

**Book Design:**
Carol Stickles

**Illustrations:**
Robert Pennise

®Rodale Press, Emmaus, Pa.

Printed in the United States of America on recycled paper, containing a high percentage of de-inked fiber.

**Library of Congress Cataloging in Publication Data**
Main entry under title:
Feasting on raw foods.
   Includes index.
   1. Food, Raw.    2. Cookery.    I. Gerras, Charles.    II. Arobone, Nancy.
TX392.F37        641.7        79-23463
ISBN 0-87857-271-6 hardcover
ISBN 0-87857-272-4 paperback

2 4 6 8 10 9 7 5 3 1 hardcover
2 4 6 8 10 9 7 5 3 1 paperback

# Contents

# Introduction

Jeff Cox, one of the editors of *Organic Gardening*® magazine, wrote an article in July of 1978 about the value of eating more raw foods on a regular basis—a lot more than most people are accustomed to eating. That article triggered an astonishing 1,200 letters from *Organic Gardening*® readers—a deluge, as these things go—cheering Jeff for focusing attention on the benefits of raw foods. Some of the correspondents were long-time fans of raw foods as a major element in the diet—among them, people who eat no cooked foods whatever. Others were new to the idea of eating raw foods that occur in any way, but as part of a salad. They wanted to know what else there is to do with raw foods and how to do it.

Clearly there were more people out there who were interested in the delights of fresh, "live" foods than any of us at Rodale Press had realized—delights of taste, of convenience, and of improved health and well-being. Some of the writers described their own raw foods regimens, along with illuminating and fascinating comments on their experiences. They sent along hundreds of favorite recipes, with instructions for preparing the kind of food they ate.

Without exception, these letter writers urged us to publish more about raw foods—not only because of their own interest in the subject, but so others could know what this way of eating can add to life. Our answer is this book—a book about an exciting way to eat that will be new to most of the people who read about it.

Sometimes in talking to friends and reading the newspapers, you get the feeling that food is on almost everyone's mind. There are those who doggedly watch their weight by carefully controlling calories and selections: some sensibly, some rashly and even foolishly. Others are waistline-deep in the traditions and rich sauces of haute cuisine. Some shun meat for religious, moral, or health reasons. Many are aware of the importance of fiber in the diet and down quantities of unprocessed bran with every meal.

There will always be those who overeat and those who don't eat enough of the nutrients they need, but in general, the public has become wiser. Consumers are learning to avoid products that have been doctored with artificial flavors and colors and those bolstered with chemical substances to make them better "shelf items."

With this greater awareness has come a heightened interest in new ways of preparing foods rich in nutrition and in truly natural flavors. One of the simplest and best cuisines of all has gone largely unnoticed and its core is literally and figuratively in our own backyard—the fresh-tasting, wonderfully nourishing, palate-tingling world of raw foods.

# "Raw" Foods Defined

What do we mean by "raw" foods? For the purpose of this book, we have chosen a definition that will make sense to newcomers to the idea of raw foods meals and be acceptable to most of those who are seriously committed to a diet high in raw foods: by "raw foods" we mean food which the cook has not heated above 140°F. in preparing it. This limit on heating is set because temperatures between 140° and 160°F. start to bring about undesirable changes in the composition of food. (The most common temperature of water from the "Hot" tap is 140°F.)

We also include some dishes which are prepared with yogurt, cheese, and gelatin—all previously cooked ingredients. Yogurt can be made from entirely raw milk, but raw milk is dauntingly difficult to find; in some states its sale is prohibited by law. Yogurt made from pasteurized (therefore, not "raw") milk is a nutritious, live food.

The reader will find many recipes that call for cheese. Most cheese is made from pasteurized milk. Raw cheeses are rare in the United States. Also, for most people, hunting up a source of raw milk and then proceeding to make their own cheese from it would be asking a lot—perhaps too much. Cheese is a healthful source of good protein, and in our opinion, its addition to our diet gives bonuses of flavor and of texture that make its pasteurized ancestry acceptable even in raw foods recipes.

Also, we will not discourage readers from buying commercial tofu (soybean cheese) or from making their own, using cooked soybeans. Even people who eat raw foods almost exclusively tend to use tofu in this form; they feel that neither the flavor nor texture of "raw" tofu is satisfactory. Tofu, even from a cooked source, is a valuable food high in protein (seven ounces supply 30 percent of a person's daily requirement for protein). For those who want to try it, we offer a recipe for Homemade Raw Tofu (see Index) from one of the readers of *Organic Gardening* ® magazine.

Unflavored gelatin appears in many recipes in this book. Made from animal cartilage, gelatin is only released when the basic raw material is cooked. You need not cook it further. It dissolves in warm water—considerably below our 140°F. limit.

Agar-agar, sometimes labeled as kanten, is a white translucent seaweed that comes in one-quarter-ounce sticks or in granular form. It also is a gelling agent for salads and desserts. Agar-agar does require further cooking at temperatures that exceed our 140°F. limit. However, as a natural source of mineral rich food and as a tool for increasing raw foods recipe variety, it is too valuable to overlook. It makes a substitute for commercial unflavored gelatin. Recipes for using agar-agar appear in the section, "Desserts."

As you might expect, many of those committed to a diet high in raw foods are vegetarians. However, for those who are not, as well as for the readers who simply would like to enhance their usual diet with a variety of raw foods, some recipes in this book contain meat and fish.

Of course everyone eats some raw foods. The salad bowl appears on almost every table, and even those individuals who never touch a leaf of lettuce will pick up an apple or banana now and then. But we are talking about experiencing the real taste excitement and variety of raw foods. This calls for expanding our horizons—going beyond the customary choices and overcoming the all too common resistance to change.

## Conditioning Counts for a Lot

In the course of preparing this book on raw foods, we talked to some people who eat raw foods almost exclusively, yet we were amazed to find that they resisted such ordinary vegetables as peas and green beans "in the raw." The lifetime acceptance of these vegetables as foods only to be cooked deprives these people not only of the good taste of tender raw peas and crisp snappy beans but keeps them from venturing even further to sample the quite elegant delights of raw Brussels sprouts, the tender sweetness of just-picked young corn on the cob, and the tang of crisp raw turnips.

Conditioning plays a large part in food choices, as we discovered in talking with a woman whose own experience ran in just the opposite direction. "My father," she told us, "ate only to still his hunger and please his palate, with never a thought to nutrition. But he introduced me, as a child, to peas straight from the pod and green beans off our backyard vine, and in more than 50 years it never occurred to me that these delicious raw vegetables were anything but ordinary snacks."

Most of the people who are experienced with raw foods as a major part of the diet advise beginners to start their raw foods regimen gradually. Later it can build to where they are eating as much as 60 percent to 80 percent of their daily food raw. Even Dr. Max Bircher-Benner, who treated patients for many years by putting them on raw foods and juices, believed that a regimen of 60 percent raw is an ideal one.

Of course there are individuals who eat almost nothing at all that has been cooked, and they are healthy and satisfied with this dietary habit. However, it is not the purpose of this book to get you to throw away all your pots and pans, forget about the Thanksgiving turkey and the good home-baked bread, and turn your back on baked potatoes and savory lentil soup. Instead, we aim to show you that your everyday meals can be enhanced by opening them to a whole new eating experience that is at once healthful, convenient, and wonderfully delicious.

# Putting Raw Foods into Your Life

part one

# Our
# Raw Foods
# Heritage

**H**umans, and prehumans before them, took their food directly from nature, finding roots and berries and the other parts of plants that experience had taught them were safe to eat. Gathering these foods regulated their lives: in the spring they would search for fresh, just ripening plants; in the summer and fall more mature fruits were the prizes; and always they moved on in the search for a new supply.

As hominids developed into *Homo sapiens* — humans as we know them today — they found the uses of fire. We don't know whether the scanty evidences of fires from almost two million years ago are traces of fires man had actually learned to make, or of coals he had taken from a natural conflagration — a forest fire, for example. But it is certain that humans have been able to control fire for more than a half million years. It made a great difference in their lives. Now, gathered around the flames, they had some light in the dark night, some warmth in the cold weather, and a place to be together, to be sociable. By then, too, our forebears were using tools, becoming hunters and fishers. Hunting led to sharing, interdependence, a more tightly knit community.

No one knows how the first humans began to cook their food. It must have happened in several different places at different times. Perhaps a piece of meat fell in the fire by accident; perhaps some curious hominid decided to see what would happen if he thrust the joint into the flames. But we do know that the enormous jaws and teeth of *Homo erectus,* believed to be man's immediate ancestor, gave way to the true human's far smaller chewing equipment. The large grinders and incisors, the powerful underslung jaw needed to grind weedy, hard plant parts and seeds and tear through the tough flesh of prehistoric animals that were such a

4

large part of the former diet were no longer necessary. Evolution favored the smaller teeth and jaw structure of modern man.

Richard Leakey, renowned anthropologist and author of *Origins* (E. P. Dutton, New York, 1977), advances a further theory about why the early humans wanted to cook their food. After pointing out they had originally been equipped to handle a raw diet, and at that stage of development it seems unlikely that taste was a consideration, Dr. Leakey surmises, "Perhaps early humans, by cooking their food, were emphasizing their specialness in the world."

Whatever the motives, it is true that the advent of fire and the consequent cooking made a change in the human animal. The supply of available foods increased; those substances that had been impossible to eat now became part of the diet. Additional protein led to larger bodies, and the fact that now there were foods that could be eaten with few or no teeth meant that people who were "old" (compared to others in the group) could survive. The overall life span was lengthened.

Remember, the raw foods that *Homo erectus* and early *Homo sapiens* lived on so long ago were not the raw foods of today. Hard seeds, stringy roots, tough leaves are a far cry from fresh, crisp, cultivated plants of today, just as raw mammoth meat must certainly have been more difficult to chew than the tender young veal of today.

Perhaps if it had stopped there, we would not be writing this book. Primitive man, by necessity, achieved a balance between the foods that he ate raw and those to which he applied the new and amazing discovery of cooking. This balance helped him refine his palate, begin to notice the differences in taste of his foods. He had gone a little beyond the stage of "eating only to survive"; food was becoming desirable for more than just a way to satisfy hunger.

# Raw Foods Were a Staple in Ancient Greece and Rome

Through the centuries the people in many places existed on diets in which raw foods dominated. The staple of poor Athenians, at the height of Athens' ancient glory, was *alphiton*, a barley-gruel for which the recipe has come down to us:

*Dry, near the fire or in the oven, twenty pounds of barley flour, then parch it in the sun. Add three pounds of linseed*

*meal, a half pound of coriander seed, two ounces of salt, and
the quantity of water necessary.*

(Gourmets enhanced this with a little millet.)

Although we know about the enormous and elaborate banquets
given by the Romans, for which master cooks concocted and served all
kinds of complex delicacies to the common people of Rome, cooking itself
was a luxury. Fuel was scarce, and very few households had any real
cooking equipment. Their ordinary diet was a raw diet: olives, raw beans
and figs, cheese, and a concoction made by stirring together pounded
grain, fat, and water. Only occasionally was there coarse bread from the
neighborhood bake shop.

*Garum,* a ubiquitous seasoning that could be made from any of a
variety of raw fish (or their entrails), brined and allowed to ferment in the
sun, was as much a staple in southern Europe as soy sauce is in China or
table salt in our own country. The Greeks, the Romans, and even their
allies in nearby Spain used it with almost everything. Particularly prized
was red mullet garum, which cost as much as the most precious perfume.

According to the 19th century London chef, Alexis Soyer, as recently
as in his own time, little more than 100 years ago, Turkish innkeepers
used garum to preserve leftover fish for subsequent meals.

In Europe of the Middle Ages, bread was a luxury; the common
people ate *frumenty,* an uncooked gelatinlike gruel made from soaked
wheat berries. In the seventh century A.D., the Chinese peasant rarely
had the means to cook his vegetables or fish; the meager supply of fire-
wood went to prepare the rice. On the Eastern European steppes, it was
not poverty but their way of life that ordained the raw foods diet of the
Mongols. They carried meat, onions, and goat milk cheese in their sad-
dlebags and ate them raw; lighting a fire would have divulged their
campsite to everpresent enemies. We can safely conclude that none of
these people knew about enzymes, vitamins, or all the other valuable
elements in food that are destroyed by cooking. They simply were re-
sponding to environmental, social, and economic conditions.

## Modern Delicacies Feature Raw Foods

Today, around the world, people are perpetuating raw foods traditions that their ancestors have bequeathed to them. For example, in Syria
and other Middle Eastern countries, people make flavorful dishes of

ground bulgur (precooked cracked wheat) mixed with onion and other flavorings and called (depending on what's in it) kibbe or tabouli. In Southeast Asia and Korea, inhabitants serve raw pickled fish with every meal, while the Japanese make their sushi from plain fresh fish and serve it with soy sauce and herbs. The Mexicans and other Spanish Americans marinate strips of raw fish in lime juice. They call the dish serviche. The Fiji Islanders call it kikoda while the residents of Tahiti call it poisson cru. One of the most elegant dishes of any country is Swedish gravad lax, salmon marinated in lemon juice and seasoned with white pepper and some salt.

Danish breakfasts often feature raw oatmeal from which the Swiss may have gotten muesli, that wonderful concoction of grain, dried fruit, and nuts. Another dish of great sophistication is the French crudite, a platter of raw vegetables, beautifully arranged and presented with a simple sauce for a dip. Not all these dishes fit our own ideas of a desirable food, since some are impossible to prepare without using a quantity of salt, which we find objectionable. However, they all certainly prove that our diets could encompass a much wider variety of raw foods than most of us eat now.

It is impossible to know what effect a diet high in raw foods had on the health of the ancients. We have only limited information about their sanitation (or lack of it), the effectiveness of their medical treatments, and the exotic foods they might have been eating — not to mention the results of heredity and the environmental conditions prevailing then — all of which played a part in the development of ancient man. Clearly, a simple cause-and-effect relationship could hardly be established.

Nonetheless, our ancestors survived somehow, and we are their heirs. Though we would not choose to return to those primitive diets featuring tough roots and leaves, there is a great attraction in the idea of exchanging the highly processed foods of today for the delicious tastes and health-giving elements our forebears enjoyed from foods eaten raw.

# Not Only Good, but Good for You!

There was a time, not all that long ago, when people generally believed that raw foods — like night air — were bad for health, even dangerous. (They also believed that wearing your overshoes indoors was bad for your eyes!) And when you weren't feeling well, your discomfort would be eased with poached eggs, creamed spinach, and the traditional chicken soup, but never, never anything raw! That notion may have resulted partly from the inadequate sanitation and refrigeration then.

Of course even then everyone ate fruit, and no doubt some farmers and gardeners were tempted by the vegetables in their garden patch to nibble a bit before the food ever got to the kitchen. But most foods — vegetables, grain, meat, and fish — were eaten cooked; fresh produce not eaten in season was "put up" in jars for the winter.

Then two things came into fashion. It became increasingly important to have a slim figure, especially for women, and for that reason or a more obscure turn of popular taste, more people began to eat salads as a regular item in their diet.

In a famous series of articles that appeared in the old *Life* magazine in the 1940s, the sociologist Russell Lynes wrote an evaluation of the various levels of American taste. In describing the large segment just behind the avant garde, he listed among many other characteristics "the cult of the rancid salad bowl." He was referring to those aficionados of the wooden salad bowl who insisted that it never be washed for fear of losing its "seasoning" but merely rubbed with paper towels or a piece of bread.

Lynes' piece was a clear indication that among chic hosts and hostesses no dinner could be considered complete without salad. The notion has since become virtually universal in the United States, as it is in most European countries.

Then, from a few "fanatics" who had been eating a high percentage of raw foods right along, the numbers began to swell until, at present, people all over the country commonly eat not only fruits and salads but raw vegetables, sprouted grains, nuts and nut butters, and lots of other good things.

We know now that those early "fanatics" were on the right track. There are important benefits to be had from adding raw foods to the diet. It all goes back to how the body processes and uses the food we eat.

# Nutrition Is Not as Simple as Firing a Furnace

More than one writer has compared the body to a furnace. "Stoke it with food," the metaphor goes. "That is the fuel. The body burns the food, making energy, just as a furnace uses coal, oil, or wood to make energy in the form of heat."

If nutrition were as simple as firing a furnace, it wouldn't matter very much what we ate; anything our bodies could "burn" — that is, combine with oxygen and convert into heat and other energy — would be fine.

But our nutrition is vastly more complicated than that. Our bodies aren't just containers for some kind of internal combustion, they are live organisms made up of some 60 trillion tiny cells. Real nutrition involves "feeding" those cells, replenishing them, replacing the ones that have died off, and speeding the waste out of our body before it can putrefy. We are sustained even when we eat foods that don't help to do this — but our tissue cells are not regenerated. We age more quickly and are not as fit as we might be. We are in what one medical researcher has called "the twilight zone" of health. We are not sick, but neither are we at a peak of well-being.

The physical process of digestion involves the cooperation of a number of our major organs. Some of them, like the stomach and the intestines, are exclusively involved with digestion. Others, like the liver, take part in digestion and a number of other body processes as well.

Digestion begins in the mouth. Our teeth are styled and arranged for cutting and for grinding; we have one bite for soft foods and another for hard — plus a built-in program that adjusts the pressure for these automatically! Teeth begin the breaking-up process of the food we eat, reducing it to small pieces that can be mixed with saliva, beginning the digestion of starches, moistening the food, and making it easier to swallow. Chewing also gives the stomach and intestines a head start on their work of reducing food to a final watery form that can be absorbed into the blood and lymph to be carried to the body cells.

Different foods spend different lengths of time in the stomach before being passed on to the intestines. Soft carbohydrates like mashed potatoes are disposed of in a matter of minutes. Meats take a longer time and leafy vegetables even longer; spinach could remain for as long as 24 hours. Fat foods slow down stomach action, and so do very cold foods like ice cream.

The intestines — with the help of enzymes from the liver and pancreas — change food into a form that the body can make use of for fuel and repair.

It is the enzymes in food and those manufactured by our own bodies that help to process fuel for energy in our body cells and make it possible for the miracle of osmosis to carry our glands' hormones between the body cells and the bloodstream.

Most nutritionists used to think that humans didn't need enzymes, because the body manufactures them. True, it does. But it doesn't manufacture all the enzymes, and it doesn't make them in the full amounts that we can profitably use. We need the enzymes that are to be found in fresh foods. With these, the energy potential of our body cells is increased.

No matter how good and fresh the food is, its enzymes cannot survive the high temperatures necessary to cook it. At temperatures over 140°F. enzymes are altered. So wisdom dictates that we not only buy or grow a good variety of food but that we spare at least some of it from the frying pan and the fire!

Enzymes, important as they are, are not the only advantage raw foods hold for our health. Raw foods contain more beneficial polyunsaturated fats. The chlorophyll in fresh greens like spinach and kale tones the heart and circulatory system and even provides a mild barrier against infection. While raw vegetables do not contain complete proteins, they have amino acids that complement those of whole grains and milk; the combination is as excellent a complete protein as anyone could wish.

# Raw Foods for Fiber

Recently the general public has become aware of the importance of fiber in the diet. Eating foods that contain substantial amounts of fiber helps us eliminate wastes quickly. Wastes allowed to remain long in the digestive system feed harmful bacteria. This brings large numbers of white corpuscles to the digestive system to fight the bacteria; their presence, however, interferes with absorption of nutrients from the food we eat. Fiber acts like a broom, sweeping the whole digestive system free of circulatory wastes and dead cells.

In 1958 Mervin Hardinge of Loma Linda University conducted nutritional, physical, and laboratory tests on 86 lacto-ovo-vegetarians (people who eat animal products only in the form of dairy foods), vegetarians (people who eat no animal products at all), and nonvegetarians. According to his findings, the pure vegetarians consumed the most plant fiber by far and the nonvegetarians the least. A diet high in raw foods, though not necessarily a vegetarian diet, is similar to it. That is, raw foods contain practically none of the refined elements so common in conventional diets, and the protein and calories in such a diet are derived mainly from foods rich in fiber — whole-grain cereals, legumes, nuts, and seeds. Also, both diets are unusually rich in fruits and vegetables.

The following table from the Agriculture Handbook No. 8 (1963), prepared by the United States Department of Agriculture, shows how cooked and raw foods differ in their content of several important types of nutrients. The original USDA table, some 60 pages, includes everything from baby food to diet cream soda. Our examples are foods that are commonly served cooked, but which are not only palatable but perfectly delicious eaten raw.

The table is good evidence that most of the vitamins and minerals in our foods suffer in the cooking pot. Also, the protein content, which sometimes increases when certain meats or fish are cooked, is less available to the body because high temperatures actually change the biochemical structure of the protein elements and make them only partly digestible. Tests conducted at the Max Planck Institute for Nutritional Research suggest that a person needs only one-half the amount of protein in his diet if he eats protein foods raw instead of cooked.

## What Will Eating More Raw Foods Do for You?

What will be the result of our eating more raw foods? Are they some kind of miraculous cure-all for disease, aging, and degeneration?

No one is claiming that. Many are experimenting with raw foods as a therapy, and a variety of theories and practices are becoming part of

[continued on page 20]

# Nutritional Difference

| Food (100 gr. edible portion) | Food Energy (cal.) | Pro-tein (gr.) | Fat (gr.) | Total carbo-hydrates (gr.) | Fiber carbo-hydrates (gr.) | Ash (gr.) | Cal-cium (mg.) |
|---|---|---|---|---|---|---|---|
| Asparagus spears, | | | | | | | |
| raw | 26 | 2.5 | 0.2 | 5.0 | 0.7 | 0.6 | 22 |
| cooked | 20 | 2.2 | 0.2 | 3.6 | 0.7 | 0.4 | 21 |
| Green beans, | | | | | | | |
| raw | 32 | 1.9 | 0.2 | 7.1 | 1.0 | 0.7 | 56 |
| cooked | 25 | 1.6 | 0.2 | 5.4 | 1.0 | 0.4 | 50 |
| Beef, round, lean, | | | | | | | |
| raw | 135 | 21.6 | 4.7 | 0 | 0 | 1.0 | 13 |
| cooked | 189 | 31.3 | 6.1 | 0 | 0 | 1.4 | 13 |
| Beets, | | | | | | | |
| raw | 43 | 1.6 | 0.1 | 9.9 | 0.8 | 1.1 | 16 |
| cooked | 32 | 1.1 | 0.1 | 7.2 | 0.8 | 0.7 | 14 |
| Broccoli spears, | | | | | | | |
| raw | 32 | 3.6 | 0.3 | 5.9 | 1.5 | 1.1 | 103 |
| cooked | 26 | 3.1 | 0.3 | 4.5 | 1.5 | 0.8 | 88 |
| Brussels sprouts, | | | | | | | |
| raw | 45 | 4.9 | 0.4 | 8.3 | 1.6 | 1.2 | 36 |
| cooked | 36 | 4.2 | 0.4 | 6.4 | 1.6 | 0.8 | 32 |
| Carrots, | | | | | | | |
| raw | 42 | 1.1 | 0.2 | 9.7 | 1.0 | 0.8 | 37 |
| cooked | 31 | 0.9 | 0.2 | 7.1 | 1.0 | 0.6 | 33 |
| Cauliflower, | | | | | | | |
| raw | 27 | 2.7 | 0.2 | 5.2 | 1.0 | 0.9 | 25 |
| cooked | 22 | 2.3 | 0.2 | 4.1 | 1.0 | 0.6 | 21 |
| Cod, | | | | | | | |
| raw | 78 | 17.6 | 0.3 | 0 | 0 | 1.2 | 10 |
| cooked | 170 | 28.5 | 5.3 | 0 | 0 | — | 31 |
| Collards, | | | | | | | |
| raw | 45 | 4.8 | 0.8 | 7.5 | 1.2 | 1.6 | 250 |
| cooked | 33 | 3.6 | 0.7 | 5.1 | 1.0 | 1.0 | 188 |
| Sweet corn, | | | | | | | |
| raw | 96 | 3.5 | 1.0 | 22.1 | 0.7 | 0.7 | 3 |
| cooked | 83 | 3.2 | 1.0 | 18.8 | 0.7 | 0.5 | 3 |

— = lack of reliable data for a substance believed to be present in measurable amount.
Adapted from Agriculture Handbook No. 8, U.S. Department of Agriculture, 1963

# Between Raw and Cooked Foods

| Phos-phorus (mg.) | Iron (mg.) | Sodium (mg.) | Potas-sium (mg.) | Vita-min A (I.U.) | Thia-mine (mg.) | Ribo-flavin (mg.) | Niacin (mg.) | Vita-min C (mg.) |
|---|---|---|---|---|---|---|---|---|
| 62 | 1.0 | 2 | 278 | 900 | 0.18 | 0.20 | 1.5 | 33 |
| 50 | 0.6 | 1 | 183 | 900 | 0.16 | 0.18 | 1.4 | 26 |
| 44 | 0.8 | 7 | 243 | 600 | 0.08 | 0.11 | 0.5 | 19 |
| 37 | 0.6 | 4 | 151 | 540 | 0.07 | 0.09 | 0.5 | 12 |
| 217 | 3.2 | 65 | 355 | 10 | 0.09 | 0.19 | 5.2 | — |
| 228 | 3.7 | 60 | 370 | 10 | 0.08 | 0.24 | 6.0 | — |
| 33 | 0.7 | 60 | 335 | 20 | 0.03 | 0.05 | 0.4 | 10 |
| 23 | 0.5 | 43 | 208 | 20 | 0.03 | 0.04 | 0.3 | 6 |
| 78 | 1.1 | 15 | 382 | 2,500 | 0.10 | 0.23 | 0.9 | 113 |
| 62 | 0.8 | 10 | 267 | 2,500 | 0.09 | 0.20 | 0.8 | 90 |
| 80 | 1.5 | 11 | 390 | 550 | 0.10 | 0.16 | 0.9 | 102 |
| 72 | 1.1 | 10 | 273 | 520 | 0.08 | 0.14 | 0.8 | 87 |
| 36 | 0.7 | 47 | 341 | 11,000 | 0.06 | 0.05 | 0.6 | 8 |
| 31 | 0.6 | 33 | 222 | 10,000 | 0.05 | 0.05 | 0.5 | 6 |
| 56 | 1.1 | 13 | 295 | 60 | 0.11 | 0.10 | 0.7 | 78 |
| 42 | 0.7 | 9 | 206 | 60 | 0.09 | 0.08 | 0.6 | 55 |
| 194 | 0.4 | 70 | 382 | 0 | 0.06 | 0.07 | 2.2 | 2 |
| 274 | 1.0 | 110 | 407 | 180 | 0.08 | 0.11 | 3.0 | — |
| 82 | 1.5 | — | 450 | 9,300 | 0.16 | 0.31 | 1.7 | 152 |
| 52 | 0.8 | — | 262 | 7,800 | 0.11 | 0.20 | 1.2 | 76 |
| 111 | 0.7 | trace | 280 | 400 | 0.15 | 0.12 | 1.7 | 12 |
| 89 | 0.6 | trace | 165 | 400 | 0.11 | 0.10 | 1.3 | 7 |

*[continued on next page]*

| Food (100 gr. edible portion) | Food Energy (cal.) | Pro- tein (gr.) | Fat (gr.) | Total carbo- hydrates (gr.) | Fiber carbo- hydrates (gr.) | Ash (gr.) | Cal- cium (mg.) |
|---|---|---|---|---|---|---|---|
| Dandelion greens, | | | | | | | |
| raw | 45 | 2.7 | 0.7 | 9.2 | 1.6 | 1.8 | 187 |
| cooked | 33 | 2.0 | 0.6 | 6.4 | 1.3 | 1.2 | 140 |
| Onions, mature, | | | | | | | |
| raw | 38 | 1.5 | 0.1 | 8.7 | 0.6 | 0.6 | 27 |
| cooked | 29 | 1.2 | 0.1 | 6.5 | 0.6 | 0.4 | 29 |
| Peanuts, | | | | | | | |
| raw (with skins) | 564 | 26.0 | 47.5 | 18.6 | 2.4 | 2.3 | 69 |
| roasted (with skins) | 582 | 26.2 | 48.7 | 20.6 | 2.7 | 2.7 | 72 |
| Peas, green, immature, | | | | | | | |
| raw | 84 | 6.3 | 0.4 | 14.4 | 2.0 | 0.9 | 26 |
| cooked | 71 | 5.4 | 0.4 | 12.4 | 2.0 | 0.6 | 23 |
| Peppers, green, immature, | | | | | | | |
| raw | 22 | 1.2 | 0.2 | 4.8 | 1.4 | 0.4 | 9 |
| cooked (boiled) | 18 | 1.0 | 0.2 | 3.8 | 1.4 | 0.3 | 9 |
| Salmon, Atlantic, | | | | | | | |
| raw | 217 | 22.5 | 13.4 | 0 | 0 | 1.4 | 79 |
| canned | 203 | 21.7 | 12.2 | 0 | 0 | 1.6 | — |
| Soybeans: mature seeds, dry, | | | | | | | |
| raw | 403 | 34.1 | 17.7 | 33.5 | 4.9 | 4.7 | 226 |
| cooked | 130 | 11.0 | 5.7 | 10.8 | 1.6 | 1.5 | 73 |
| sprouted, | | | | | | | |
| raw | 46 | 6.2 | 1.4 | 5.3 | 0.8 | 0.8 | 48 |
| cooked | 38 | 5.3 | 1.4 | 3.7 | 0.8 | 0.6 | 43 |
| Spinach, | | | | | | | |
| raw | 19 | 1.1 | 0.1 | 4.2 | 0.6 | 0.6 | 93 |
| cooked | 14 | 0.9 | 0.1 | 3.1 | 0.6 | 0.4 | 93 |
| Sweet potatoes, | | | | | | | |
| raw | 102 | 1.8 | 0.7 | 22.5 | 0.9 | 1.0 | 32 |
| cooked | 141 | 2.1 | 0.5 | 32.5 | 0.9 | 1.2 | 40 |

| Phos-phorus (mg.) | Iron (mg.) | Sodium (mg.) | Potas-sium (mg.) | Vita-min A (I.U.) | Thia-mine (mg.) | Ribo-flavin (mg.) | Niacin (mg.) | Vita-min C (mg.) |
|---|---|---|---|---|---|---|---|---|
| 66 | 3.1 | 76 | 397 | 14,000 | 0.19 | 0.26 | — | 35 |
| 42 | 1.8 | 44 | 232 | 11,700 | 0.13 | 0.16 | — | 18 |
| 36 | 0.5 | 10 | 157 | 40 | 0.03 | 0.04 | 0.2 | 10 |
| 29 | 0.4 | 7 | 110 | 40 | 0.03 | 0.03 | 0.2 | 7 |
| 401 | 2.1 | 5 | 674 | — | 1.14 | 0.13 | 17.2 | 0 |
| 407 | 2.2 | 5 | 701 | — | 0.32 | 0.13 | 17.1 | 0 |
| 116 | 1.9 | 2 | 316 | 640 | 0.35 | 0.14 | 2.9 | 27 |
| 99 | 1.8 | 1 | 196 | 540 | 0.28 | 0.11 | 2.3 | 20 |
| 22 | 0.7 | 13 | 213 | 520 | 0.08 | 0.08 | 0.5 | 128 |
| 16 | 0.5 | 9 | 149 | 420 | 0.06 | 0.07 | 0.5 | 96 |
| 186 | 0.9 | — | — | — | — | 0.08 | 7.2 | 9 |
| — | — | — | — | — | — | — | — | — |
| 554 | 8.4 | 5 | 1,677 | 80 | 1.10 | 0.31 | 2.2 | — |
| 179 | 2.7 | 2 | 540 | 30 | 0.21 | 0.09 | 0.6 | 0 |
| 67 | 1.0 | — | — | 80 | 0.23 | 0.20 | 0.8 | 13 |
| 50 | 0.7 | — | — | 80 | 0.16 | 0.15 | 0.7 | 4 |
| 51 | 3.1 | 71 | 470 | 8,100 | 0.10 | 0.20 | 0.6 | 51 |
| 38 | 2.2 | 50 | 324 | 8,100 | 0.07 | 0.14 | 0.5 | 28 |
| 47 | 0.7 | 10 | 243 | 9,200 | 0.10 | 0.06 | 0.6 | 23 |
| 58 | 0.9 | 12 | 300 | 8,100 | 0.09 | 0.07 | 0.7 | 22 |

public awareness. Dr. John M. Douglass of the Southern California Permanente Medical Group in Los Angeles has records of diabetic patients whose need for insulin has been greatly reduced since he put them on a diet that is mostly raw foods.

In Massachusetts, Dr. Ann Wigmore treats terminal cancer patients at her Hippocrates Health Institute with a wide variety of entirely raw foods — including sprouted grains, seedling greens, juices, and a ferment of soaked wheat called, encouragingly, "Rejuvelac."

Viktoras Kulvinskas is working along similar lines in Connecticut. He has worked with Dr. Wigmore. His ideas about nutrition, backed by research in medical literature, are presented in detail in his book, *Survival into the 21st Century: Planetary Healers Manual* (Omangod Press, Wethersfield, Conn., 1976).

In Switzerland, for over 60 years the clinic founded by Dr. Max Bircher-Benner has been treating patients from all over the world for arthritis and allied disorders. The treatment is based on a diet that is about 60 percent fresh juices and raw foods. Through experience Dr. Bircher-Benner arrived at that approximate percentage as the ideal one to bring about and maintain health. When certain physical conditions must be corrected, the clinic recommends a 100 percent raw foods diet for a limited time.

In describing the work at the clinic, Dr. Bircher-Benner noted the experiments that were conducted with top young athletes in Germany by a Dr. Karl Eimer. At the peak of their training, Dr. Eimer had the athletes gradually change over to a purely raw foods diet from their usual regime of high-fat and high-protein foods. The food was strictly supervised, and the young men's metabolism and athletic achievements were also monitored. The researcher found that there was no lessening of athletic prowess. The athletes were able to eat and assimilate the necessary amount of food, and their sports performance actually improved during the raw foods period.

Dr. Paavo Airola, in his book *How to Get Well* (Health Plus Publishers, Phoenix, Ariz., 1978), says a 100 percent live food regime would be the best for treatment of disease and for everyday bodily maintenance. However, he concedes that few of us live in an environment that continually provides us with fruits and vegetables so fresh that none of the nutritive value is lost in shipping and handling. He therefore recommends eating most of our foods raw — perhaps 80 percent — particularly most fruits, vegetables, nuts, and seeds and filling out the diet with a small amount of lightly cooked vegetables, some of the legumes like beans and peas, and some grains.

## An Impressive Success Story

At the individual level, Betty Crowder from Oroville, California, has been a "raw fooder" for more than 25 years. This music teacher, a widow and grandmother, credits her raw foods diet with the fact that for 20 years she has not had one of the grand mal epileptic seizures that frequently plagued her up to that time. "I was known in just about every hospital in San Francisco," she says. "They never could find the reason for my seizures. Then on one of my periodic trips to the emergency room, a neurotherapist said to me, 'You'd better be careful of your diet; you could get diabetes.' I'd been reading everything I could get my hands on about epilepsy, but then I started looking up works about diet and vitamins. I became more and more convinced that this was the key.

"Finally, one day I went out and ate all the things I loved — pie a la mode, chocolate cake, ice cream — and from then on, I cut them all out completely. I've been living for years on raw fruits and vegetables, nuts and seeds."

Miriam Meppelink, a young mother in Michigan, says that since beginning her present diet pattern three years ago — almost all raw foods: nuts, sprouts, seeds, fruits, and vegetables — she has not been troubled by a previously recurrent bladder infection, insomnia, and some less specific physical complaints that had plagued her. "Not only that," she says, "but I feel better in many other ways. I'm happier, more peaceful, more joyful. I find that I smile a lot more!"

Research in raw foods is still going on. All its properties will not be known for some time. For that reason, different people working in different areas of interest have conflicting theories about how much of the diet should be raw. Nonetheless, all these researchers agree that for better nutrition and health everyone should include a significant percentage of raw foods in his or her diet.

# Introducing Raw Foods at Your House

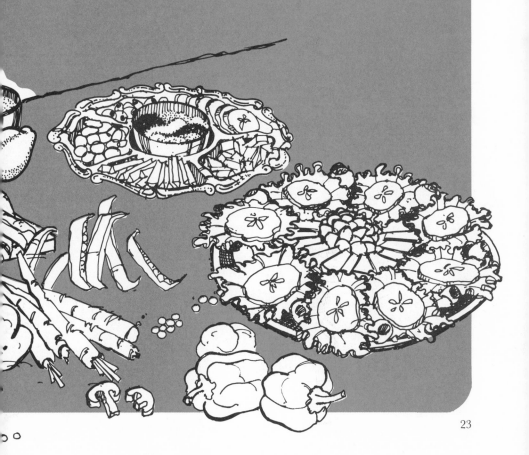

**P**icture yourself in an elegant restaurant, a true temple of fine food. You are sitting with your companions at a table covered with a white linen cloth and adorned with a centerpiece of fresh flowers, at each place an exquisite setting.

The waiter brings you the first course. The menu describes it as "Belgian endive wheels *au Brie.*" Following that comes *gazpacho,* the famous Spanish cold soup. It is garnished with *crudite,* raw vegetables cut into tiny diamonds and julienne strips, and chopped peanuts.

Now the main course — *filet de sole aux limon* — filet of sole marinated in herb-seasoned lemon juice, then wrapped around a stuffing of chopped fresh mushrooms, garnished with red and white radish flowers. With the sole is *burgul aux aumonds* — soaked wheat grains flavored with slivered almonds — and a *salade* of cress, cucumber, and tiny, crunchy alfalfa sprouts, all in a delicious dressing.

Top it all off with *coeur a la creme* for dessert, an elegant finale for an impressive repast.

Doesn't that sound grand? Certainly it's far more than a run-of-the-mill meal! Yet everything on that menu is uncooked, and recipes for dishes just like these are in this book.

But perhaps you're not interested in elegant gourmet food. You may be planning a party for teenagers, many of whom have been just about living on hamburgers, pizza, cola, and french fries. You want to give them a meal that doesn't violate the principles of good nutrition, but you don't want to disgrace your own children by making their parents seem "different." Most young people are reasonable, and you should do well with, for instance, "sandwiches" that use raw spreads as fillings and slices of good

24

cheese or crisp cucumber as their "bread." Add some cheese chunks, fruit and nuts, and several fruit juice drinks to round out the menu.

We're out to prove that more raw foods in your life don't have to mean depressing platters heaped with unlikely plant life that you are expected to chomp your way through as though you were grazing a meadow. This is a new cuisine. And just as meals can be made more fun by trying dishes from foreign countries, you can add to the interest and variety of the food you serve by starting with the recipes in this book and working into entire meals of uncooked or, as some nutritionists say, "unfired" foods.

How to start? There should be nothing drastic about this, and much will depend, of course, upon your household's eating habits and willingness to accept a few changes.

In some families, a first step might be to discuss the matter beforehand with the people who share your meals. In others, a deadpan "dinner is served" approach may be more effective. That is up to you.

Now make a list of the raw foods your household eats regularly without even thinking about it.

Then go through this book and pick out a few recipes you think your own family would particularly enjoy.

Make and serve one of the dishes. If it is accepted with pleasure, and "the pudding proved by the eating," try another recipe the following week. As long as things go smoothly, you can step up the incidence of raw foods on the menu unobtrusively. This gradual approach is better for the system, too. Your body needs a chance to adjust gradually to a new form of nourishment. This is particularly true of raw foods with their high roughage content.

Having a garden is a big help. Jeff Cox, the *Organic Gardening*® editor whose article on raw foods sparked this book, says he, his wife, and their young children rarely sit down in the house to an evening meal during the summer growing season. They just go out into the garden and eat! Good growing things can tempt even the most die-hard, and just-picked vegetables can go far in filling out anyone's summer menu.

## Make It Look Good!

Consider the way you present your uncooked dish. It should be, first of all, attractive to look at. How food is cut is one way to establish the look of your dish, and it also makes an enormous difference in the way it seems to taste, how it feels in the mouth, and in a diner's attitude toward the dish itself. A very little boy we know "orders" his lunch as he is leaving for school. He is very careful to specify "a peanut butter sandwich cut into triangles" or "a peanut butter sandwich cut into squares," as though, indeed, they were entirely different kinds of sandwiches. And to him they really are.

The Chinese are aware of the importance of how the ingredients in a dish are cut. In *Jim Lee's Chinese Cookbook* (Harper & Row, New York, 1968), the author tells us that a dish with exactly the same components but differently cut (like our young friend's peanut butter sandwiches) may be listed five different times on a Chinese menu as though each were a different recipe altogether.

Esther Milburn, who has been involved in the food preparation at the holistic-healing Beechwold Clinic in Columbus, Ohio, says that one of the favorite dishes there is her "ring salad," an enormous platter blazing with the colors of a variety of vegetables. The outer ring is made of bright-orange shredded carrots. Next comes a ring of dark-red beets. Mrs. Milburn uses white jicama or, when that exceptionally good Mexican vegetable is not available, cauliflower or turnips for a ring of white. Inside that, a ring of sprouts and then beans or lentils. In the center she provides four or five different homemade dressings. Mrs. Milburn quotes the well-known nutritionist and iridologist, Dr. B. Jensen, in noting that if you make a point of eating food of every color, you are almost sure to be eating a balanced diet.

Certainly nothing contributes to the appeal of food more than contrasts of color. Magazines show that they are well aware of it by publishing the enticing color photographs they do in both their articles and advertisements.

There are tips and tricks on presenting food interestingly and attractively, and we share them with you throughout. Look at the directions for preparing the Antipasto Plate (see Index) or the Fresh Fruit Dips (see Index) for some good ideas.

Then, of course, the taste and its cousin, the aroma, are crucial to the dishes you prepare. In a later chapter we will talk about buying the ingredients for your raw foods dishes, but let us assume that you have bought the freshest-smelling, best-tasting foods you could find. Right there you are off to a head start — just as you would be with any cooked dishes for which you have the finest ingredients. But now you won't have to risk spoiling that good fresh flavor by overheating or "drowning" it.

# Seasoning Really Counts

How to enhance the fresh, natural flavor? The recipes suggest judicious use of seasonings and garnishes that combine tastes for contrast, complement, and health. For example, tofu, mixed with carefully chosen herbs, makes a savory, high-protein dressing. In various international recipes we combine traditional native ingredients with additions high in food quality, such as nuts, sprouts, and cheeses, to arrive at dishes that are both nutritious and flavorful.

You will notice, too, that the ingredients themselves are often more than just ordinary foods. The many cheese dishes call for the better-flavored, unprocessed imported and top American products that extend one's range of taste as they contribute to a satisfying and nourishing dish.

As your household gradually begins eating a larger and larger percentage of uncooked food, you will begin to appreciate some of the happy by-products of a quasi-raw foods program. While you will probably have to spend as much time preparing the food you are to serve as you do any other — cleaning it, peeling it, slicing or cutting or grating it — you will find the total meal preparation task very much easier and quicker. And cleaning up afterward becomes a breeze.

In the first place, of course, you will eliminate all the cooking time. While "cooking time" with some foods is merely "put it in the oven and forget it," much more often it requires the cook to keep at least one eye on the simmering pot or sizzling pan. With raw foods, you can forget that chore. And another plus — no need to start preparing a meal far enough in advance to allow for cooking time.

When you have eaten and it is time to clean up, you will realize that you have used a hearteningly small number of utensils compared to those you must use when you cook and that they are much easier to clean. There are no pots with burnt-on food, no pans full of grease. Everything can go in the dishwasher or requires just a rapid swoosh with a soapy sponge or brush and a rinse.

In planning to adjust your menus, remember that raw foods come to the table cool or cold. To gauge the amount of these you should include in the beginning, consider the climate and the time of year. On a freezing winter day in Boston it takes a great deal of idealism and trust to willingly join in a sudden switch from warm to cold foods.

The Beechwold Clinic sets as a goal for the food programs it provides its patients a minimum of 50 percent raw food in winter and 60 percent in summer. Their food pattern specifies that on two days a week the individual eat no flesh foods and emphasize vegetables, yogurt, cheese, and salads instead. On the other five days, although various cooked foods are called for, salads and other fresh foods bring the percentage up to the desired minimum.

If cooked foods are served at the end of the meal, they will be required in far less quantity, and still the diners will leave the table feeling satisfied. In time your family will learn that the "full" feeling that comes after eating a heavy cooked meal is less an indication that they are no longer hungry than it is that they have filled their stomachs with an unnecessary bulk.

Remember that raw fruits require totally different enzyme combinations than raw vegetables do. Mixing these two types of food may result in digestive upsets for some people. If you are one of these, try eating these foods separately. Lemon, papaya, and avocado are known to be compatible with all types of foods.

If there are fatties at your house, they are sure to notice that as they eat more uncooked foods they are losing some of those extra pounds. On raw foods you eat less and your body operates more effectively with the amount of food it gets. Your cells function more efficiently, both within themselves and with regard to one another, and this allows you to eat less, get rid of extra weight, and still feel and be at the peak of fitness!

# Will the Kids Eat This Way?

If you are distressed because the young people in your household tend to eat between-meal snacks that are at best simply nonnutritious, at worst downright harmful, you can make it easier for them to switch to the right ones. Keep a big bowl of mixed seeds, nuts, and dried fruits handy, and the kids will be less likely to go down the street for a candy bar. Have cleaned vegetables in the refrigerator, ready to be made into a satisfying nosh between meals with a couple of whacks with a knife.

You can't have absolute control over what older children are eating, but habit and example go a long way. If the little ones are raised on this kind of snacking, it will reinforce good food habits in them later.

Suppose all this works, and that the recipes in this book "take," and suppose you find you enjoy raw foods and have a feeling of physical well-being since you began eating more of them. But you work during the day, which means you are away from your home at lunchtime. Perhaps there is neither a natural foods restaurant nor a salad bar near your workplace, or if there is, perhaps you cannot afford to patronize it regularly. How do you manage? No matter where you go to buy your lunch, you can probably get some sort of salad. If it is really impossible, brown-bag it using the "sandwiches" in this book — Rye-Ricotta Sandwich Filling (see Index) or Almond-Vegetable Spread (see Index) on tomato, for example. They are certainly the foundation of an excellent lunch, and you can vary them as you wish. Also, if you have a little space near a window in your workplace, big enough to accommodate a quart jar on its side, you might even want to set up a sprout garden. In the section, "Growing for the Table," we show you just how to do it.

Social occasions may present a bit more difficulty if you are eating a very high percentage of raw foods. Play the situation by ear. You know the people close to you. It would be nice if you could depend on them to respect what you are trying to do and to realize that when you refuse

some of the things they serve it is no reflection either on their cooking or their hospitality. They are likely to be so sweetly reasonable as to provide a special salad for you. If they do not want to be tolerant, however, you must decide whether good relations are worth a temporary lapse in your raw foods diet.

In any case, it is wise not to act as though you are the only one who has The Word. With that attitude, there is the inescapable impression that you are pitying everyone else for the dreadful state of health they are in because they haven't the sense to know how to eat — as you have! Be gentle, be tactful, be respectful of differences of opinion. Don't make a federal case out of the matter. Relax in the knowledge that you are doing what you feel is best — for you!

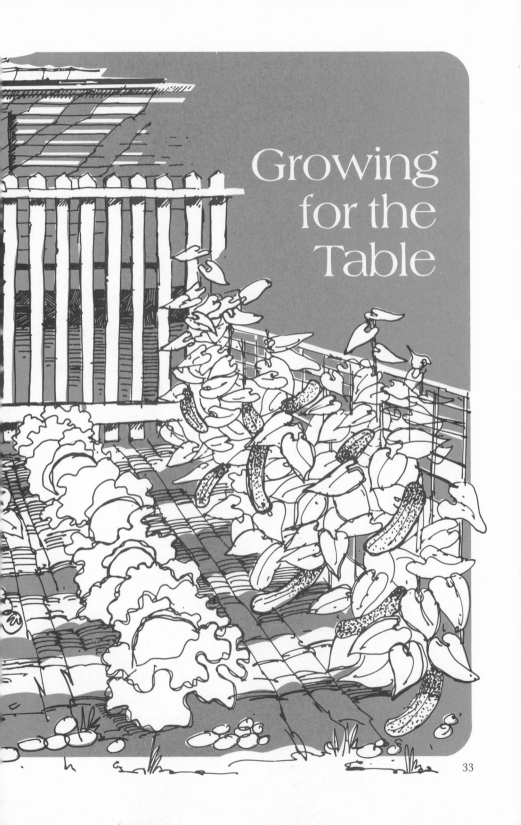

Growing
for the
Table

33

$\text{T}$hose in the very best position to start eating more uncooked foods are the lucky ones with flourishing gardens. They have the most tempting delicacies just outside the door — at least for a few months of the year.

What about the large numbers of Americans who are apartment dwellers, with no land to call their own? Is there any way that they, too, can enjoy food they have grown themselves?

One movement that seems to be taking hold, to the benefit of apartment dwellers with a yen to garden, is communal gardening. An unused plot of land is divided among several people, to be cultivated for the season. In some communal gardens plotholders plant their individual area the way they choose; in others the entire garden is a communal affair, with everyone sharing in the planning, the work, and the harvest.

Of course we know there are many good books that tell the beginner how to garden. But in a book about raw foods, we believe there should be a few tips about overcoming the handicap of winter weather or lack of land and suggestions for how to get the benefit of at least some of your own produce in an apartment or landless home, in or out of season.

The first place to turn, of course, is to sprouts, those truly miraculous little goodies of the plant world. Amazingly simple to grow, sprouts can be raised almost anywhere at any time and by anybody. The cost is practically nil — the starting seeds, beans, or grains themselves and some basic equipment. Who can't rustle up an old wide-mouth jar or two, a bit of fine screening or cheesecloth, a rubber band or mason jar ring, and a brown paper bag? Sprouts take only a few days from start to harvest, a time during which vitamin content can increase 700 percent!

Sprouts are, in a sense, like eggs; each seed contains the embryo of a plant and also a supply of food to enable the plant to grow until the roots

34

it has developed are mature enough to take nutrients from the soil. They are rich in almost every important mineral. They have vitamins A, B, C, and E in genuine abundance and impressive amounts of protein. What's more, the proteins in many sprouts have been turned into amino acids — "predigested," as it were — during the time the little plants are bursting out of the mother seed. They also furnish us with the enzymes we need more and more as we get older. Yet sprouts have very few calories — certainly few enough so that any dieter need not hesitate to eat his or her fill of them.

Best of all, sprouts are delicious! Each variety of sprout has its own taste and its own texture. Some like wheat are sweet; cress sprouts are peppery; mung are crunchy and mild. They are good individually or in combination, and sprouts not only enhance sandwiches, salads, and main dishes, but they make a delightful snack or side dish by themselves.

# Directions for Sprouting

How do you sprout? It's very simple.

First, it's best to get the kinds of seeds, beans, or grains that are meant for sprouting — from a natural foods store, from some supermarkets or groceries, or by mail order. Your local nursery or supply house may have "seed quality" seeds for sprouting; be sure to get seeds that have not been treated with spoilage retardant, insecticides, or preservatives. Even so, when you get them home, wash them well. Seed quality seeds will germinate better than those primarily intended for eating, but if the latter is all you can get, sprout them.

Some of the things you can sprout: alfalfa, radish, and sesame seeds, legumes (beans including mung, soy, kidney, lima, navy, garbanzo, pinto, and lentil, plus peas and peanuts), unpearled barley, unhulled millet, whole oats, rye, and wheat. There are many others. Look around. (Do not sprout tomato or potato seeds. Their sprouts are poisonous when eaten in quantity, and not good in any amount.)

Here is the simplest way to sprout — a way that is just as effective as any other. Let's assume you are beginning with mung beans (although the procedure is the same for any sprouts). Get a one-quart, wide-mouth jar and make a cover for it with a piece of fine screening, cheesecloth, or nylon net. (How fine your mesh cover has to be depends on the size of the seed or bean you are sprouting. You can use a much wider mesh for big seeds like mung beans; for tiny alfalfa seeds, you will want a cover with tinier holes.) Use a rubber band on the cheesecloth or other mesh to fix the cover over the mouth of the jar. If your container is a preserving jar, you can substitute a jar ring without the center disk for the rubber band.

Though special kits are sold for growing sprouts, the homemade way seems to be perfectly satisfactory for most people. A quart jar is not by any means the only container you can use. You can sprout in crocks, bowls, casseroles — anything made of either glass or ceramic (not metal or wood) that has a wide opening and room for your beans to spread out when the jar is laid on its side.

Wash one-quarter cup of seeds or beans under running water and put them in the container (less if using small seeds such as alfalfa). Cover them with one cup of lukewarm water. This will make about one cup of

sprouts. Let the beans soak overnight — at least 8 hours in summer and about 12 in winter.

Drain the beans very well, pouring the water out right through the cover. You may want to save the sprout water (it's very nutritious) to use in preparing food, to drink, or to water your plants with.

Rinse the beans with fresh cool water, swishing it around gently, and drain well. Now, while the plant is in the process of emerging from its kernel, put the jar into a paper bag, or in a dark, somewhat warm place like the enclosure under a kitchen sink. Let it stand for two or three days, rinsing the beans two to three times a day. At the end of that time, the sprouts should be just about as long as the beans from which they sprang and they are ready to eat.

If you'd like your sprouts to have a nice tinge of green, take the jar out of the bag, or its dark hiding place, when the sprouts are full grown and expose them to the sun for a few hours. In this way you release the chlorophyll from the plants. Sun-warmed alfalfa sprouts are as beautiful in texture and color as they are nutritious.

People without gardens, or those whose gardens are buried under ice and snow for almost half the year, can enjoy fresh sprouts all around the calendar. Try the different kinds. Try growing two or more different sprout varieties together, so that they come up ready-mixed.

Sprouts will keep a few days in a plastic bag in your refrigerator. They can be frozen for a few months, although they will no longer be crisp when you defrost them. They can be dried in a food dryer, an oven, or in the sun and then ground into a kind of flour or malt that you can use as a partial substitute for other flours or a sweetener.

# Growing Other Vegetables in the House

You can grow other vegetables besides sprouts to enliven your meals during the long winter months. Since indoor gardening takes more work and time than growing the wonderful sprout, take stock of which greens you can easily find in satisfactory condition and at a reasonable price in local stores, then plan to grow others that are not so readily available elsewhere.

You will need:

## Light

Indoor plants should have six to eight hours of natural sunlight a day or an artificial light source. There are special lamps under which to grow plants, but many indoor gardeners successfully use a combination of inexpensive warm and cool fluorescent tubes. Rig your lights (or, alternatively, your plant table) so that the tops of the plants can always be about four inches below the light source; as they grow, you'll need either to raise the light or lower the plant!

If Old Sol is your light source, be sure to shield the plants from the heat of the direct rays. Put up slatted blinds, venetian blinds, or gauzy curtains as a barrier against the burning rays of the sun coming through glass.

## Even Temperature

Depending on the particular plant, you will need a growing atmosphere between 50° and 60°F.

## . . . and Humidity

Indoor winter air is very dry (unless you have a humidifier). You can achieve a proper humidity level in various ways: by a daily misting of

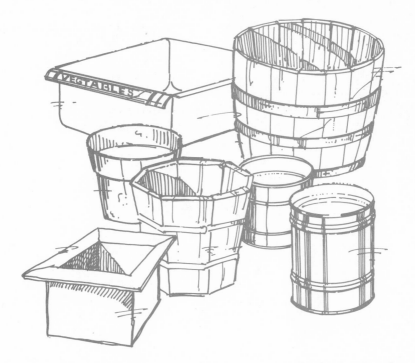

your plants, by setting the pots on pebbles over water, by putting damp sphagnum moss under clay flowerpots.

## Containers

Depending on many factors — space, the time you have to spend, how much you want to grow in your indoor garden — you can use almost any kind of container. Vegetable crispers from an old refrigerator, old barrels sawed in half, pots of all kinds, largish baskets lined with plastic (punch some holes in the plastic), window boxes, apple or orange crates (also lined with punctured plastic) — all will do. Or try smaller containers like the bottom of a half-gallon or gallon milk carton, plastic bleach bottles with the tops cut off, large cans (although eventually these will rust). Look around, use your imagination, and you won't have to spend a lot of money on containers for your plants. Just be sure the container is deep enough — at least eight or nine inches.

## Soil

Potting soil, adjusted for the particular plants you are growing, is fine. You may want to add sand, vermiculite, peat moss, or compost. If you use garden soil, bake it in the oven at 350°F. for one to one-and-a-half hours to kill insects, weeds, and destructive fungi.

## Water

Give your plants a drink of lukewarm water often, but not so much that the soil becomes soggy. Leafy vegetables need water once a day, fruiting vegetables every other day. Feed them with "instant compost" every two weeks or so. To make it, liquefy vegetable scraps in water in the blender and apply it to the plants. Include eggshells and coffee grounds if you have them, but no flesh. Work any solid residue into the soil.

## Fresh Air

Your plants need it, especially in winter-heated houses. Yet you must be careful to protect them from drafts, which can be fatal. Help them breathe — keep leaves clean and don't have plants crowded close

together. On those inevitable unseasonably warm days, open a window in a room away from the "garden," where the cold air can't blow directly on it, and air the house a bit. (Not, however, to the point where you over-work the furnace.) Failing a warm day, try putting a circulating fan — the kind used to cool rooms in summer — at a discreet distance from the plants and running it for a half hour or so every now and then. It won't pull in air from the outdoors, but it will stir up the air in the house, which is a fairly adequate substitute.

# What to Grow

Common sense tells you that you don't want giant plants or sprawly ones in an indoor garden.

You can grow any number of leafy vegetables: garden lettuce, Boston lettuce, romaine, endive, spinach, chicory . . .

And you also can have your crop of fruiting vegetables. Cucumbers do well in a sunny window; tomatoes (especially the tiny cherry tomatoes), green peppers — all are easy to care for and make excellent indoor "farm produce." Be careful not to overfeed them, or they will turn into luxurious foliage plants without a fruit in sight.

You can even raise a supply of root vegetables; radishes, carrots, and beets should do well indoors.

And don't forget herbs, including the potherbs like parsley, which are windowsill crops par excellence.

Try to space your plantings so that when one crop has been harvested, another is just coming in ready to be picked. This is the ideal; you may not have the space to have so many things growing at once, but at least aim for a steady supply of your homegrown vegetables. Do what you can . . .

. . . and don't forget to grow sprouts!

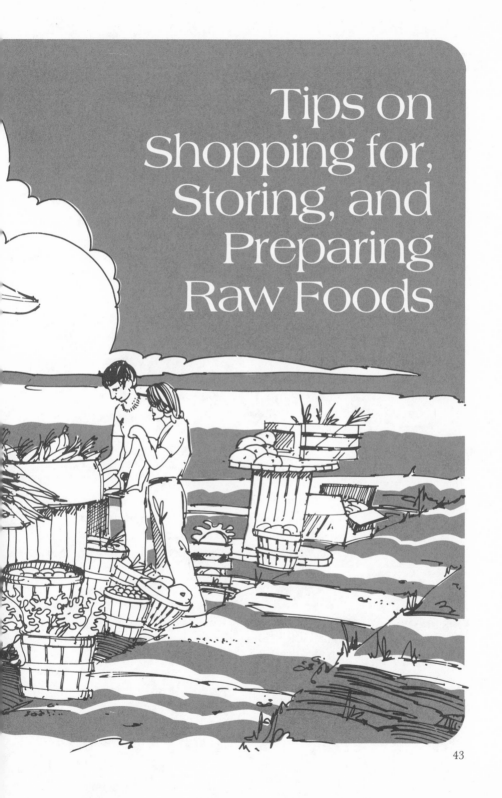

# Tips on Shopping for, Storing, and Preparing Raw Foods

**R**aw foods recipes utilize a bounty of produce, and you'll want it to be as fresh as possible to ensure the best taste, the highest nutrient content, and the most pleasing appearance. If you grow all your own produce, consider yourself blessed. If not, check the yellow pages of the telephone directory under "Grocers" where you are likely to locate suppliers you never knew existed in your community.

Acquaint yourself with neighborhood ethnic shops. They commonly stock ingredients that might be difficult to obtain in a supermarket. Italian stores always have fennel, oregano, garlic, sweet basil, olive oil, wine vinegar, dried mushrooms, freshly grated Parmesan, Romano, asiago cheese (a delicious substitute for Parmesan). Some even offer homemade ricotta cheese, a firmer and sweeter variety than supermarket brands, and it is sold loose. Around Christmastime your Italian grocer might even surprise you with whole imported carob bean pods, also known as Saint-John's-bread.

Oriental food stores generally carry tofu, raw peanuts, soy sauce, rice vinegar, seaweed products, fresh sprouts, dried mushrooms, and some unusual varieties of produce. Look to the Latin grocers for plantains, guavas, and sweet onions, the Greek ones for feta cheese and olives, and the Slavic stores for their special paprika, poppyseed, and dill.

## Consider the Co-ops

Food cooperatives are springing up in many communities. People gather together to buy wholesome fresh food at close to wholesale prices and from as many direct sources as they can find. Such foods include grains, oils, herbs, nuts, seeds, dried fruits, dairy products, natural sweeteners, organic produce, and flours. Some cooperatives are loosely formed and made up of a few families or individuals who more or less "share" shopping chores. Many of the larger ones function almost like a retail store where nonmembers can buy whatever is available but must pay more than members who invest time and energy in the operation.

Usually members pay a very small yearly membership fee and provide a service such as selling and packaging or cleaning the store for perhaps two hours a month, or they might visit suppliers to pick up the foods that are to be sold. The "service" one woman provided for her cooperative was to teach her rather well-known bread-baking course to approximately 10 other members.

Food cooperatives are listed in your telephone book. Call and visit several if you can; one may appeal to you more than another. Consider joining; there are so many advantages: top-quality foods at a good price, an opportunity to share ideas with people who refuse to accept the status quo in consumerism, and possibly a chance to learn something new, like bread baking, preserving, or a useful craft from another member.

Farmers markets go hand in hand with the raw foods chef. Usually they're open only on certain days and during certain seasons. Shop these markets early in the day if you want to get the pick of the crop. Take a quick but discerning stroll through the entire market before making any purchases. Shop for the best product at the best price. Strike up a conversation with the salesperson who may be a member of the farming family that grew the food.

The selection is diverse. Besides produce, the assortment might include meats, fish, cheese, nuts, dried fruits, and sweeteners. But just because you're in a farmers market, don't assume that everything for sale is grown or made in your area. Ask about sources and purchase locally grown foods whenever possible. They'll be fresher, and you'll be supporting your local farming community. Also, chances are that their products won't contain the preservatives, fungicides, or ripening agents added to products that are shipped long distances.

In the summer and fall take a ride into the countryside and see for yourself what freshly picked produce is available at the local roadside stands. Some farmers allow you to pick your own. Try it — the kids will love doing it and everyone will be especially appreciative of that harvest. Look in the classified section of your newspaper for notices about pick-your-own orchards and farms. You might also find ads from local dairies that sell certified raw milk products and eggs. Feel free to call your County Cooperative Extension Service (listed in the white pages) about any food-related question. This agency has a wealth of information and is supported by your tax dollars.

Your plans for serving a particular fruit or vegetable can determine the condition and appearance of the produce you decide to purchase. If it's to be served whole or as a garnish, the "look" is important. But a few blemishes, hailstone marks, insect or bird nibbles won't matter if the product is to be chopped or ground and combined with other ingredients.

# Get the Most Out of Fresh Produce

Freshness, however, is essential. If fruits and vegetables look shriveled or if leafy greens are wilted, you can be certain that a great deal of their food value is gone. Try to buy your produce loose rather than prepackaged. It allows you the freedom to choose the size, quality, and quantity that you want.

Everyone sets personal price guidelines and limits on spending, but one good rule is to avoid buying out-of-season items. Not only is the cost

prohibitive, but flavor and texture are seldom at their best. The following produce chart will be helpful to you in planning your purchases. It gives you an idea of how to foresee prices and quality of certain fruits and vegetables at various times of the year.

# Monthly Availability Expressed as Percentage of Total Annual Supply

| Commodity | Jan. % | Feb. % | Mar. % | Apr. % | May % | June % | July % | Aug. % | Sept. % | Oct. % | Nov. % | Dec. % |
|---|---|---|---|---|---|---|---|---|---|---|---|---|
| **Apples,** *all* | 10 | 9 | 10 | 9 | 8 | 5 | 3 | 4 | 9 | 12 | 10 | 11 |
| *Washington* | 10 | 11 | 11 | 11 | 11 | 7 | 4 | 2 | 5 | 8 | 9 | 11 |
| *New York* | 10 | 10 | 12 | 11 | 9 | 6 | 2 | 2 | 7 | 11 | 10 | 10 |
| *Michigan* | 13 | 12 | 12 | 10 | 6 | 2 | * | 2 | 5 | 13 | 12 | 13 |
| *California* | 6 | 6 | 7 | 5 | 2 | 1 | 4 | 15 | 26 | 15 | 8 | 5 |
| *Virginia* | 9 | 8 | 8 | 5 | 2 | * | 1 | 2 | 16 | 19 | 17 | 13 |
| **Apricots** | | | | | 11 | 60 | 27 | 2 | | | | |
| **Artichokes** | 4 | 6 | 14 | 19 | 12 | 5 | 6 | 7 | 5 | 8 | 8 | 6 |
| **Asparagus** | * | 6 | 28 | 31 | 20 | 10 | * | * | 1 | 1 | 1 | |
| **Avocadoes,** *all* | 9 | 7 | 8 | 8 | 8 | 7 | 7 | 8 | 7 | 9 | 11 | 11 |
| *California* | 7 | 8 | 11 | 10 | 10 | 10 | 8 | 8 | 6 | 6 | 8 | 8 |
| **Bananas** | 8 | 8 | 10 | 9 | 8 | 8 | 7 | 7 | 7 | 8 | 9 | 9 |
| **Beans, snap,** *all* | 6 | 4 | 6 | 9 | 10 | 12 | 12 | 11 | 9 | 8 | 7 | 6 |
| *Florida* | 12 | 9 | 14 | 20 | 14 | 3 | * | | * | 2 | 12 | 14 |
| **Beets** | 5 | 5 | 6 | 6 | 6 | 12 | 14 | 13 | 12 | 10 | 7 | 4 |
| **Berries, misc.**\*\* | | | | | 2 | 30 | 39 | 14 | 8 | 5 | 2 | |
| **Blueberries** | | | | | 1 | 26 | 43 | 28 | 2 | | | |
| **Broccoli** | 10 | 9 | 12 | 9 | 9 | 7 | 5 | 5 | 7 | 9 | 9 | 9 |
| **Brussels sprouts** | 13 | 13 | 12 | 7 | 4 | * | | 2 | 6 | 14 | 17 | 12 |
| **Cabbage,** *all* | 10 | 8 | 9 | 9 | 9 | 9 | 8 | 7 | 7 | 8 | 8 | 8 |
| *Florida* | 17 | 15 | 19 | 22 | 15 | 3 | * | | * | 1 | 8 | |
| *Texas* | 16 | 14 | 18 | 12 | 8 | 3 | 2 | 2 | 1 | 3 | 8 | 13 |
| *California* | 10 | 9 | 11 | 9 | 11 | 11 | 7 | 6 | 5 | 7 | 7 | 7 |
| *New York* | 9 | 7 | 5 | 3 | 1 | 1 | 7 | 10 | 12 | 16 | 17 | 12 |
| *North Carolina* | 1 | | | * | 11 | 27 | 9 | 10 | 9 | 8 | 17 | 8 |
| **Cantaloupes,** *all* | | * | 3 | 4 | 10 | 20 | 25 | 22 | 11 | 4 | 1 | |
| *California* | | | | | * | 15 | 28 | 33 | 16 | 6 | 1 | * |
| *Mexico* | | 1 | 17 | 32 | 43 | 7 | | | | | | |

*[continued on next page]*

| Commodity | Jan. % | Feb. % | Mar. % | Apr. % | May % | June % | July % | Aug. % | Sept. % | Oct. % | Nov. % | Dec. % |
|---|---|---|---|---|---|---|---|---|---|---|---|---|
| Texas |  |  |  |  | 23 | 47 | 19 | 9 | 1 | * |  |  |
| Arizona |  |  |  |  | * | 48 | 47 | * |  | 4 | * |  |
| **Carrots,** all | 10 | 9 | 10 | 9 | 8 | 7 | 7 | 7 | 7 | 9 | ,9 | 8 |
| California | 9 | 8 | 8 | 8 | 10 | 11 | 11 | 8 | 6 | 6 | 7 | 8 |
| Texas | 15 | 16 | 18 | 16 | 8 | 3 | * | 2 | 2 | 3 | 7 | 9 |
| **Cauliflower,** all | 9 | 6 | 8 | 7 | 6 | 6 | 5 | 6 | 9 | 15 | 14 | 9 |
| California | 10 | 7 | 10 | 10 | 9 | 8 | 6 | 6 | 6 | 8 | 10 | 10 |
| **Celery,** all | 9 | 8 | 9 | 8 | 8 | 8 | 8 | 7 | 7 | 8 | 10 | 10 |
| California | 8 | 6 | 7 | 7 | 7 | 10 | 9 | 7 | 7 | 9 | 13 | 10 |
| Florida | 15 | 15 | 17 | 15 | 14 | 8 | 1 |  |  | * | 3 | 11 |
| Michigan |  |  |  |  |  | 1 | 20 | 29 | 30 | 16 | 3 | 1 |
| **Cherries, sweet** |  |  |  |  | 11 | 41 | 43 | 5 |  |  |  |  |
| **Chinese cabbage** | 10 | 9 | 8 | 8 | 8 | 8 | 7 | 8 | 8 | 9 | 9 | 8 |
| **Coconuts** | 9 | 7 | 9 | 7 | 6 | 5 | 4 | 7 | 8 | 8 | 11 | 19 |
| **Corn, sweet,** all | 3 | 2 | 4 | 7 | 16 | 17 | 16 | 14 | 8 | 5 | 5 | 3 |
| Florida | 5 | 4 | 6 | 11 | 27 | 24 | 5 | * | * | 5 | 7 | 6 |
| California |  |  |  |  | 10 | 27 | 25 | 17 | 9 | 7 | 4 | * |
| New York |  |  |  |  |  |  | 5 | 45 | 40 | 10 |  |  |
| **Cranberries** |  |  |  |  |  |  |  |  | 8 | 26 | 48 | 18 |
| **Cucumbers,** all | 7 | 5 | 6 | 7 | 11 | 12 | 12 | 9 | 8 | 8 | 8 | 7 |
| Florida | 4 | 1 | 2 | 10 | 29 | 11 | 1 |  | * | 7 | 21 | 13 |
| Mexico | 23 | 21 | 23 | 15 | 2 | * |  |  |  |  | 2 | 13 |
| California | * | * | 1 | 3 | 12 | 15 | 21 | 17 | 13 | 10 | 6 | 2 |
| **Eggplant** | 10 | 8 | 8 | 9 | 7 | 7 | 8 | 10 | 9 | 8 | 8 | 8 |
| **Escarole-endive** | 10 | 9 | 10 | 10 | 9 | 8 | 7 | 7 | 6 | 7 | 8 | 9 |
| **Garlic** | 8 | 8 | 8 | 8 | 8 | 8 | 10 | 9 | 10 | 9 | 7 | 6 |
| **Grapefruit,** all | 12 | 12 | 12 | 11 | 10 | 6 | 4 | 3 | 3 | 8 | 10 | 9 |
| Florida | 11 | 12 | 13 | 13 | 11 | 5 | 2 | * | 3 | 10 | 10 | 10 |
| Texas | 18 | 18 | 18 | 11 | 4 | * |  |  | * | 5 | 11 | 14 |
| Western | 5 | 5 | 6 | 7 | 12 | 15 | 17 | 16 | 10 | 2 | 2 | 3 |
| **Grapes** | 4 | 3 | 3 | 3 | 2 | 6 | 11 | 17 | 18 | 15 | 10 | 8 |
| **Greens*** | 10 | 9 | 11 | 10 | 9 | 7 | 6 | 6 | 7 | 8 | 8 | 9 |
| **Honeydews** | 1 | 1 | 3 | 5 | 7 | 12 | 10 | 20 | 22 | 15 | 3 | 1 |
| **Lemons** | 8 | 6 | 8 | 8 | 9 | 11 | 11 | 9 | 7 | 8 | 7 | 8 |
| **Lettuce,** all | 8 | 7 | 9 | 9 | 9 | 9 | 9 | 9 | 8 | 8 | 8 | 7 |
| California | 8 | 8 | 8 | 7 | 10 | 10 | 10 | 9 | 9 | 9 | 7 | 5 |
| Arizona | 11 | 6 | 13 | 25 | 7 | 1 | * | * | * | 2 | 13 | 21 |

| Commodity | Jan. % | Feb. % | Mar. % | Apr. % | May % | June % | July % | Aug. % | Sept. % | Oct. % | Nov. % | Dec. % |
|---|---|---|---|---|---|---|---|---|---|---|---|---|
| *Florida* | 16 | 15 | 20 | 16 | 9 | * | | | | * | 8 | 15 |
| *Ohio* | 6 | 6 | 9 | 7 | 6 | 8 | 12 | 12 | 9 | 9 | 9 | 7 |
| **Limes** | 6 | 4 | 5 | 5 | 9 | 12 | 13 | 12 | 10 | 8 | 7 | 9 |
| **Mangoes** | * | 1 | 3 | 6 | 17 | 23 | 28 | 17 | 4 | 1 | | |
| **Mushrooms** | 9 | 8 | 9 | 9 | 9 | 8 | 7 | 7 | 7 | 8 | 9 | 9 |
| **Nectarines** | * | * | * | | 1 | 19 | 36 | 30 | 12 | * | | |
| **Okra** | 2 | 3 | 6 | 7 | 11 | 14 | 17 | 17 | 11 | 7 | 3 | 2 |
| **Onions, dry,** *all* | 9 | 7 | 8 | 8 | 9 | 9 | 9 | 9 | 8 | 9 | 8 | 7 |
| *Texas* | 1 | * | 4 | 26 | 27 | 14 | 12 | 10 | 3 | 1 | 1 | 1 |
| *California* | 3 | 1 | 1 | 1 | 11 | 21 | 23 | 17 | 8 | 6 | 5 | 3 |
| *New York* | 12 | 9 | 11 | 6 | 2 | 1 | 1 | 8 | 14 | 13 | 12 | 11 |
| **Onions, green** | 7 | 6 | 8 | 10 | 11 | 10 | 10 | 8 | 7 | 7 | 7 | 7 |
| **Oranges,** *all* | 11 | 12 | 13 | 11 | 10 | 7 | 5 | 4 | 4 | 5 | 8 | 10 |
| *Western* | 9 | 10 | 12 | 12 | 11 | 7 | 5 | 5 | 6 | 6 | 7 | 10 |
| *Florida* | 14 | 15 | 14 | 11 | 9 | 6 | 3 | 1 | 1 | 4 | 9 | 13 |
| **Papayas, Hawaii** | 6 | 6 | 6 | 7 | 10 | 10 | 9 | 8 | 8 | 10 | 11 | 9 |
| **Parsley & herbs****** | 8 | 7 | 9 | 7 | 7 | 8 | 7 | 8 | 8 | 9 | 11 | 11 |
| **Parsnips** | 12 | 11 | 11 | 9 | 7 | 5 | 3 | 4 | 8 | 11 | 10 | 9 |
| **Peaches,** *all* | * | * | | | 6 | 17 | 31 | 29 | 15 | 1 | | |
| *California* | | | | | 8 | 22 | 34 | 24 | 10 | 2 | | |
| *South Carolina* | | | | | 1 | 19 | 53 | 26 | 1 | | | |
| *Georgia* | | | | | 5 | 42 | 45 | 8 | | | | |
| *New Jersey* | | | | | | | 8 | 54 | 37 | 1 | | |
| **Pears,** *all* | 7 | 7 | 7 | 6 | 4 | 2 | 4 | 13 | 16 | 17 | 10 | 7 |
| *California* | 1 | * | * | * | | | 12 | 33 | 27 | 20 | 5 | 1 |
| *Washington* | 9 | 9 | 8 | 6 | 2 | | | 9 | 16 | 16 | 14 | 11 |
| *Oregon* | 16 | 16 | 13 | 7 | 1 | | | * | 3 | 15 | 16 | 13 |
| **Peas, green** | 12 | 12 | 13 | 13 | 12 | 12 | 10 | 6 | 5 | 2 | 1 | 2 |
| **Peppers,** *all* | 8 | 7 | 8 | 7 | 8 | 10 | 11 | 9 | 9 | 8 | 8 | 7 |
| *Florida* | 15 | 9 | 10 | 14 | 16 | 14 | 1 | | | * | 6 | 15 |
| *California* | | | | * | 2 | 7 | 13 | 15 | 20 | 28 | 14 | 1 |
| *Mexico* | 19 | 24 | 25 | 13 | 5 | 2 | 1 | 1 | 1 | 1 | 2 | 6 |
| **Persimmons** | | | | | | | | | | 33 | 48 | 19 |
| **Pineapples** | 7 | 7 | 11 | 10 | 12 | 12 | 9 | 7 | 6 | 5 | 7 | 7 |
| **Plantains** | 7 | 7 | 6 | 8 | 8 | 9 | 9 | 11 | 10 | 9 | 6 | 10 |
| **Plums-prunes** | * | * | * | | 1 | 15 | 33 | 32 | 15 | 2 | | |
| **Pomegranates** | | | | | | | | 2 | 9 | 72 | 15 | 2 |
| **Potatoes,** *all* | 9 | 8 | 9 | 8 | 9 | 8 | 8 | 8 | 8 | 9 | 8 | 8 |
| *California* | 5 | 5 | 5 | 4 | 9 | 23 | 23 | 9 | 5 | 4 | 4 | 4 |

[continued on next page]

| Commodity | Jan. % | Feb. % | Mar. % | Apr. % | May % | June % | July % | Aug. % | Sept. % | Oct. % | Nov. % | Dec. % |
|---|---|---|---|---|---|---|---|---|---|---|---|---|
| *Idaho* | 13 | 12 | 13 | 13 | 13 | 7 | 1 | * | 1 | 6 | 10 | 10 |
| *Maine* | 13 | 12 | 15 | 17 | 15 | 5 | * | * | 1 | 3 | 8 | 10 |
| *Colorado* | 12 | 10 | 12 | 1 | 7 | * | * | 6 | 9 | 11 | 10 | 11 |
| *North Dakota* | 15 | 13 | 14 | 12 | 5 | 1 | * | * | 2 | 9 | 14 | 14 |
| **Pumpkins** | 1 | 1 | 2 | 2 | 2 | 2 | * | * | 3 | 83 | 2 | 1 |
| **Radishes** | 8 | 8 | 10 | 11 | 11 | 8 | 8 | 7 | 6 | 6 | 9 | 8 |
| **Rhubarb** | 8 | 15 | 16 | 23 | 21 | 9 | 3 | 1 | 1 | 1 | 1 | 1 |
| **Spinach,** *all* | 9 | 9 | 11 | 9 | 9 | 8 | 7 | 6 | 7 | 8 | 8 | 9 |
| *California* | 9 | 10 | 12 | 10 | 9 | 7 | 7 | 7 | 6 | 7 | 8 | 8 |
| **Squash,** *all* | 8 | 6 | 6 | 7 | 8 | 9 | 10 | 9 | 9 | 11 | 10 | 7 |
| *California* | 4 | 3 | 3 | 8 | 10 | 12 | 11 | 10 | 10 | 13 | 11 | 5 |
| *Florida* | 11 | 9 | 11 | 15 | 15 | 3 | * | 1 | 1 | 6 | 14 | 14 |
| **Strawberries,** *all* | 3 | 5 | 8 | 18 | 29 | 16 | 7 | 5 | 4 | 2 | 1 | 2 |
| *California* |  | * | 3 | 22 | 35 | 18 | 9 | 6 | 4 | 2 | * | * |
| *Mexico* | 21 | 25 | 29 | 5 |  |  |  |  |  | * | 5 | 14 |
| **Sweet potatoes,** *all* | 9 | 8 | 8 | 7 | 5 | 3 | 3 | 5 | 9 | 11 | 19 | 13 |
| *North Carolina* | 9 | 8 | 10 | 10 | 7 | 4 | 1 | 1 | 6 | 12 | 19 | 13 |
| *Louisiana* | 9 | 8 | 9 | 6 | 2 | * | 5 | 11 | 11 | 11 | 16 | 12 |
| *California* | 8 | 7 | 8 | 8 | 5 | 4 | 3 | 3 | 7 | 10 | 20 | 17 |
| **Tangelos** | 23 | 4 | * |  |  |  |  |  |  | * | 33 | 39 |
| **Tangerines** | 21 | 8 | 7 | 4 | 2 | * |  |  | * | 5 | 20 | 32 |
| **Tomatoes,** *all* | 7 | 6 | 8 | 8 | 11 | 11 | 11 | 9 | 7 | 8 | 7 | 7 |
| *California* | 1 | * |  | * | 1 | 8 | 17 | 16 | 16 | 22 | 13 | 5 |
| *Mexico* | 13 | 17 | 22 | 20 | 16 | 5 | * | * | * | * | 2 | 3 |
| *Florida* | 14 | 8 | 10 | 12 | 20 | 13 | * | * |  | * | 6 | 17 |
| *Ohio* |  |  | 1 | 6 | 18 | 20 | 24 | 11 | 5 | 6 | 7 | 2 |
| **Turnips & rutabagas** | 12 | 10 | 10 | 8 | 6 | 4 | 4 | 6 | 7 | 11 | 13 | 9 |
| *Canada* | 11 | 10 | 9 | 7 | 3 | 1 | 1 | 4 | 10 | 12 | 19 | 13 |
| **Watermelons** | * | * | 1 | 3 | 10 | 28 | 31 | 20 | 5 | 1 | * | * |

* Supply is less than 0.5% of annual total.
** Mostly raspberries, blackberries, and dewberries.
*** Includes kale, kohlrabi, collards, cabbage sprouts, dandelion, mustard and turnip tops, poke salad, bok choy, and rappini.
**** Includes also parsley root, anise, basil, chives, dill, horseradish, and others.
By United Fresh Fruit and Vegetable Association by Charles E. Magoon

Store perishable items in the proper place as soon as you get them home. Even a short time in a warm dry room will exact its toll on dairy products and leafy produce. In fall and winter store appropriate fruits and vegetables in a cool cellarway or shed where temperatures do not reach freezing. Allow items that are not yet ripe to mature at room temperature, then refrigerate. In spite of popular lore, this practice should include bananas. After they are as ripe as you like, store them in the refrigerator. The skins will turn brown, but the bananas will neither get riper nor softer.

Most fruits and vegetables keep better dry than moist. Don't wash them until you are ready to use them. Berries and grapes are particularly susceptible to rotting if first washed and then refrigerated.

Salad greens are a special case. Frequently cooks talk about how they make certain to keep the endive, romaine, Swiss chard, spinach, and escarole leaves dry to avoid serving a limp salad. In truth, too-dry leaves will absorb the dressing and that can really make a salad flat!

Actually the crispness in greens comes from the moisture in their leaves. One way to ensure this crispness is to wash the greens and put them in a large colander to drain. If the leaves are large, like romaine, stand them on end so that they drain well. If you wish to store them intact, layer them between terrycloth towels and roll the layers of towels and leaves like a jelly roll. Secure the roll and refrigerate it until you are ready to use it. This takes advantage of the moisture the refrigerator provides, plus whatever moisture is left on the leaves; the towels prevent moisture from lying on the leaves and rotting them.

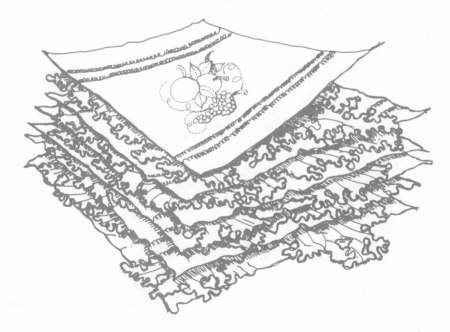

A simpler method for crisping greens and getting a head start on the salad is to wash and then drain a fairly large quantity of greens. While they are still slightly wet, break serving-size pieces of the greens into a large plastic container. At this point you can add other vegetables that hold up fairly well — coarsely chopped red cabbage and shredded carrots, for example. Cover greens with a damp paper towel and cover the container with a tight-fitting lid. The greens should remain in an excellent state for at least 24 hours.

## How to "Hold" Produce

Freezing is an excellent way to preserve produce for juicing and for blending or chopping into various uncooked sauces, soups, and casserole combinations. Most instructions for freezing tell you to freeze fruits in

sugar and to blanch most vegetables before storing them in the freezer. You don't have to do either. One of the best food-freezing tips that we know of came from a devoted gardener. She taught us to freeze tomatoes in season au natural; wash and dry them, place them in plastic bags, exhaust as much air from the bags as possible, seal the bags with twist-ties, and pop them in the freezer. Plan to use them in sauces, cold soups, and the like. You will find that they taste more like fresh tomatoes than those preserved any other way.

As an alternative to freezing food to preserve it, many kinds of fruits and vegetables can be dried. Just put the food out in the sun (properly shielded from insects). You can also use a very low oven, or an electric dryer — a boxlike contraption with slide-in shelves made of screening. Food is spread out on screened shelves, the electricity is turned on to maintain an even low heat, and the food is gradually and steadily dehydrated. After drying, it will keep for a very long time in plastic bags or other airtight containers. A note of caution: be sure the food is thoroughly dry before removing it from the dryer, then store it in a place where it will not become damp. Aflatoxin, a harmful fungus, can grow in foods not thoroughly dried before storage.

If you have the facilities, you can keep the root vegetables and sturdy fruits like apples for quite a long time the way our forebears did — in the equivalent of a "root cellar." You will need a cool, but not freezing,

dark place. Store the food so that air can circulate around it, or bury carrots, beets, potatoes, and other root vegetables in clean sand.

Parsley is the only fresh herb that consistently appears on the produce shelves. In season, a grocer will occasionally stock dill, anise, and basil if any are available from suppliers. Generally, however, you do not find variety and freshness unless you grow your own. In our section, "Growing for the Table," we give instructions on ways to grow herbs indoors. When you harvest these fresh herbs with the intent to use them soon, keep recently harvested herbs in a moisture-proof bag or with their "feet" in a jar of water, like cut flowers, with a plastic bag over the top. Either way, keep them in the refrigerator.

# Preserving Herbs

You can freeze herbs or dry them for future use. If you freeze basil leaves, first sprinkle them with a little olive oil. To hang-dry herbs, tie the stems together in moderate-size bunches and hang them upside down in

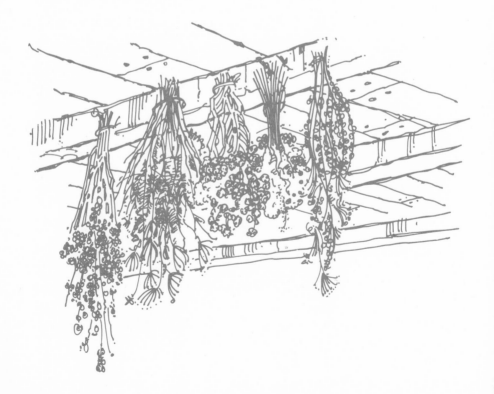

a dry place; the attic or a barn is ideal. You can also spread herbs on a wooden frame and dry them out of doors, but you must take them in before evening dew and not put them out again until the morning dew has evaporated. You can dry herbs in a food dryer, too, or on screens in a 150°F. oven. To separate these dry leaves from their branches, fill a paper bag with several bunches of one type, tie the bag closed, and shake. Store the leaves in an airtight glass jar in a dry, not overly heated area.

# Nuts at Their Best

Most people believe that when they buy nuts in their shells they obtain the freshest ones available. This is true if the nuts are freshly harvested. If you don't have time for shelling nuts, seek a source for newly shelled fresh ones. Food cooperatives and retailers usually buy from a dried fruit and nut distributor who sells and replenishes his stock quickly. Look in a telephone book for the name of a distributor from whom you might be able to buy directly. Be certain the nuts you buy are raw, not roasted and salted. You may also be able to buy some seeds at the same distribution source.

When preparing a recipe with nuts, don't hesitate to use another kind if you're not fond of the one listed or if it is unavailable. For example, black walnuts are a treat for some people, but taste unpleasantly bitter to others. You can substitute English walnuts or any other nutmeat in their place. Filberts and almonds are sometimes difficult to chop or grind; if your patience wanes quickly, substitute those nuts with softer meats like walnuts, pecans, and even Brazils, which may look tough but are real "smoothies."

Keep unshelled nuts in a cool place, like a cellar; keep shelled ones in a covered container in the refrigerator. They can be frozen either way. With shells, they will keep in plastic bags in the freezer for a year. If they are shelled, nuts will last four to six months in the freezer, enclosed in airtight, moisture-proof bags.

If you find that buying an increased quantity of nuts has too much of an adverse effect on your budget, try substituting sunflower seeds for some of the quantity of nuts specified in a recipe. Grind the seeds along with the nuts. It is almost impossible to detect the substitution. The texture and mild taste of the seed resembles that of most nutmeats, but during some seasons the cost of hulled seeds is sometimes one-fifth of that of some shelled, high-priced nuts.

# If You Serve Raw Meat or Fish . . .

If you intend to prepare raw beef, lamb, or veal, patronize a reliable butcher who guarantees that the meat is absolutely fresh and of good quality. Insist on meat that is untreated with chemicals and comes from animals that have been raised on unsprayed feeds. Such meat is not easy to find. Shop at natural foods stores for the meat. If your store doesn't stock it, ask for information on a good source. Sometimes a friend who keeps sheep or cows will sell some of his meat. Occasionally a butcher selling meat from animals raised on his own land is able to assure you that the product is as pure as possible.

Look for beef that is fine grained with rosy flesh and creamy white fat. Lamb should be bright pink with young, moist bones showing red at the joints. Darker meat, with larger, drier-looking bones, signals the older, tougher mutton.

The ideal veal is milk fed. Most of this is sold to restaurants, although you may be able to find it at specialty butcher shops. The flesh of a milk-fed calf is smooth, firm, and velvety, a pale grayish pink. The bones are soft and reddish. Older veal that has been weaned and fed on grain has pink to light red meat and young-looking bones. Veal is always fat-free.

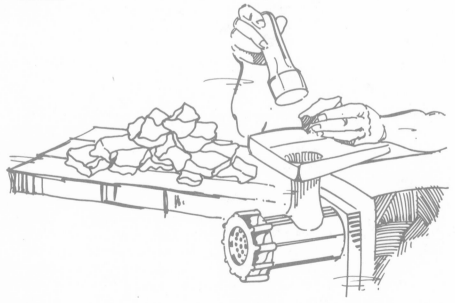

Most of the raw meat you eat will be ground or chopped, but don't ever buy it that way. Get it whole or in chunks. It will keep fresher in that form until you are ready to use it. Wrap it loosely and store it in the refrigerator with room for air to circulate around it. Put it in the freezer about a half hour before grinding it. Grind the meat just before you are about to use it. Do not handle it any more than is necessary.

If you plan to eat raw fish, use only freshly caught saltwater fish unless you are able to get fresh fish from what you know is pure water. Sadly, there is too much pollution in most of our lakes and streams to take the risk of eating raw freshwater fish from an unknown source.

Fish must be absolutely fresh. Japanese restaurants that regularly serve sushi buy from the fishing boats when they come in to shore. Some of the larger Japanese restaurants keep their sushi fish swimming around in tanks until they are ready to prepare the dish.

If you cannot buy your fish at the shore or catch it yourself, select wisely at your local fish market. Look for fish with bright bulging eyes and tightly overlapping scales. Very fresh fish have bright blue eyes with gold around the iris. The eyes become sunken and dull when the fish is not fresh.

A fresh fish will look moist and firm. If you poke it with an inquiring finger, you will meet some resistance; the flesh will be resilient and springy. The gills will be red under the gill flaps. If the fish is large, and the merchant has cut it into slices or steaks, the flesh that shows at the cut should be shining and translucent without discoloration.

As a further check, pick up the fish, lift the gill cover, and sniff. A briny salt-air smell means a fresh fish; a "fishy" odor indicates that this fish has been around for a while and would not really be welcome in your home or on your table. Have something else for dinner.

If you do come home with a lovely fresh fish, take care of it until it is time to eat it. Protect it from the loss of any of the moisture that makes it so delicious. Remove it from the merchant's wrapping and store it tightly wrapped in a plastic bag in the refrigerator. When it is time to prepare the fish, do not wash it unless it is absolutely necessary; then quickly do so in cold water and dry it immediately with paper towels.

Most people do not realize that cooking simply coagulates the protein in fish just as it does in the whites of eggs. Marinating in lemon (or lime) juice according to the directions in the section, "Main Dishes," will produce a texture much closer to cooked fish than you might expect.

# Cheeses and Cultured Milk Products

Dairy products are incorporated into many raw foods recipes. Let personal preference be your guide when selecting hard cheeses if you are not fond of the kind the recipe calls for. The softer Roquefort and blue cheeses are quite salty, have a similar crumbly texture, contain a blue-green mold, and can be used interchangeably. Feta is also salty.

Some recipes in this book leave it up to you to use either yogurt or sour cream. Results will be similar but not the same. Sour cream will produce a firmer, richer product. It will contribute more fat, while yogurt will add more protein. A recipe for Homemade Yogurt appears in the recipe section under "Breakfast."

Two other cultured milk products, piima and kefir, are also useful in raw foods preparation. Sometimes, in recipes they are interchangeable with each other, with milk, or with yogurt.Both culture without the use of heated milk.

Yogurt is available everywhere, whereas kefir and piima are not so easy to come by. In the section, "Beverages," we give directions for making kefir and piima and addresses where you can order starters for the latter two if you cannot find them in your local natural foods stores.

When buying creamed cottage cheese, check the label carefully. You might not want the added flavors, emulsifiers, and preservatives. Be wary of similar additives in half-and-half, light, heavy, and whipping creams, particularly those marked ultrapasteurized. The fat content of creamed cottage cheese differs according to what has been used to cream the dry skim milk curd. It could be cream, or whole or skim milk. You might want to cream your own cottage cheese by adding about half as much yogurt, cream, or milk to dry curd cheese.

Dry curd cottage cheese, sometimes referred to as popcorn or pot style, is not always easy to find. One of the reasons might be that its shelf life is short. It molds quickly, especially if unsalted.

Ricotta is a whole milk cottage cheese, moister and sweeter than its skim milk cousin.

Tofu is a high-protein, nondairy soybean "cheese" made from the curd of soymilk. The Oriental food stores usually carry a soft and hard curd. The soft contains more moisture and is easiest to use in recipes calling for mashed tofu; the hard is easiest to use in those that call for cubes. Store tofu covered with cold water in a closed plastic container or glass dish. Drain the water each day and replace with fresh water. This method will keep tofu fresh for several weeks.

Ideally, eggs should come from "fertile, free-running chickens," a facile phrase becoming almost as popular as "natural foods." You must always be a wary consumer. Try to find a farmer or distributor who can guarantee that the hens have been raised on natural feed in a natural environment.

The only difference between brown eggs and white is color. Never buy cracked-shell eggs for use in raw foods recipes; there will be no heating to destroy any dangerous bacteria which might have invaded the shell. Refrigerated, fresh eggs will be good for as long as three weeks.

# The Preferred Oils

We'd like to suggest that you buy "cold-pressed" vegetable oil to use in these recipes, but the truth is that presses for expressing oil from seeds and fruit kernels at temperatures below 160°F. are no longer in operation. The best choice these days is a product that is extracted by pressure several times greater than the original cold-pressed method. Such oil is often labeled as "cold-pressed, unrefined," but the more accurate labels say only "unrefined." This oil still contains lecithin, fatty acids, chlorophyll, and carotenoids (vitamin A).

Most natural foods stores and food cooperatives carry good quality oils. These are most commonly extracted from safflower, sunflower, and sesame seeds, soybeans, peanuts, and the germ of whole-grain corn. Look for deep color, sediment in the bottom of the bottle, and a smell and color that you recognize as characteristic of the basic ingredient.

Because of the large number of soybeans that this country produces, soy oil is usually a good buy, and safflower oil is never much more expensive. Olive oil is always expensive, and the unrefined kind is rather strong-tasting for some palates. You might choose to mix it with another kind of oil.

Occasionally a discriminating store will stock "crude" oils. These are good quality oils which are even less processed than their unrefined shelf mates. You will recognize them immediately because they are dark, and their smell is a strong reminder of the oil smell of the original product. Crude soybean oil, for example, has a nutty flavor. One-eighth to one-quarter cup in a quart of salad dressing made with a less obvious-tasting oil will produce wonderful results.

To store good oil, keep it in a cool place, preferably the refrigerator. Use it within a reasonable amount of time to avoid rancidity.

# Uncooked Grains

Even by themselves, the soaked grains called for in these recipes are a rich source of protein, but combine them with dairy products and legumes, particularly, and you have a source of complete protein. The following summary of complementary protein relationships will help you to balance your meals to get the fullest benefit not only from grains but from other food combinations as well.

In selecting grains, you have a long list from which to choose: wheat, rye, corn, rice, oats, buckwheat, barley, millet, and triticale. Triticale is a relatively new strain of grain, a cross between wheat and rye. Some nutritionists say that this grain contains approximately 16 percent more protein than most other cereal grains. It is also a closely balanced protein source — close to that in eggs and meat.

Most grains are available from natural foods stores, food cooperatives, and in bulk from flour and grain mills. Some kinds come in a variety of guises. Wheat, for example, comes whole in the form of "berries," cracked, flaked, ground into a meal and, of course, further ground into flour.

For utmost freshness in those recipes, buy whole grains. If the grains, as they appear in these recipes, are too coarse to suit your palate, grind the grain finer. (Some grains will break down in a blender or coffee grinder, for others you will need a grain mill.) Grind grain shortly before using it so that the oils in the germ stay fresh as long as possible. Realize that the soaking time for ground grains will be shorter. (See the Index for instructions on "How to Prepare Soaked Whole Grains.")

Store grains in a cool dry place or in the refrigerator or freezer. Use grains within a reasonable amount of time; unrefrigerated, they should keep their nutritional value for at least four to six weeks.

An ingredient that many of us take for granted when considering flavor and health is water. Try springwater for a decided difference in purity and flavor if your regular supply is chlorinated or foul-tasting.

# Some Useful Extras

Certain ingredients common to many recipes and certain techniques deserve special note. For example, an array of herbs and spices are included, some of which you may never have tried before. Pay attention to the suggested amounts, but then feel free to vary the amounts according

[continued on page 62]

# Summary of Complementary Protein Relationships

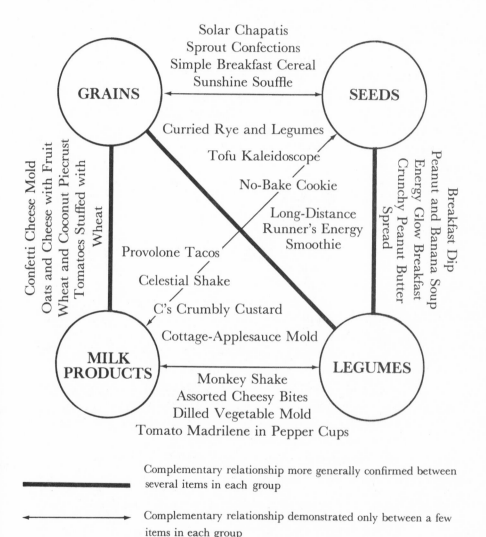

Solar Chapatis
Sprout Confections
Simple Breakfast Cereal
Sunshine Souffle

GRAINS ← → SEEDS

Curried Rye and Legumes

Tofu Kaleidoscope

No-Bake Cookie

Long-Distance
Runner's Energy
Smoothie

Provolone Tacos

Celestial Shake

C's Crumbly Custard

Cottage-Applesauce Mold

Confetti Cheese Mold
Oats and Cheese with Fruit
Wheat and Coconut Piecrust
Tomatoes Stuffed with
Wheat

Breakfast Dip
Peanut and Banana Soup
Energy Glow Breakfast
Crunchy Peanut Butter
Spread

MILK PRODUCTS ← → LEGUMES

Monkey Shake
Assorted Cheesy Bites
Dilled Vegetable Mold
Tomato Madrilene in Pepper Cups

▬▬▬▬▬▬   Complementary relationship more generally confirmed between several items in each group

◄――――――►   Complementary relationship demonstrated only between a few items in each group

Adapted from *Diet for a Small Planet* by Francis Moore Lappé

The menus are made from the raw foods recipes in this book.

to your own taste. If you're unsure of a seasoning, add it last. Start with a small amount and increase it gradually if you choose, or substitute a seasoning with which you feel more comfortable. If you're substituting a dry herb for fresh, the rule is to use half as much of the dry. When the amount called for is small, the difference in moisture is insignificant. However, if the fresh herb is a major ingredient, rehydrate the dried leaves in water overnight. Drain and use.

All soy sauces are not the same. Most of the widely used brands contain corn syrup and caramel coloring. A truly superior product is tamari soy sauce made of soybeans, wheat, salt (approximately 18 percent), and water. Like good wine it is not "green"; it has been aged in wooden casks for two years. It has a strong, rich taste; you do not need much to achieve an effect. Most natural foods stores carry the product.

In this book we occasionally list nut butters in recipes for certain beverages and spreads. They are pastes made from ground nuts which contain enough oil to make a spreadable consistency. Some contain additional oil.

Tahini and sesame butter, high-protein seed pastes common to Middle Eastern cooking, enhance the taste of particular dressings, sauces, spreads, desserts, and confections. Tahini is the product of crushed, hulled sesame seeds. You whisk water into it to extend the tahini or to liquefy it as it becomes dry and hard with age.

Sesame butter from unhulled sesame seeds is darker and more nutritionally valuable than tahini, but you use it in the same way.

We give a recipe for making peanut butter in the section, "Dips, Sandwiches, Fillings, and Spreads." You can substitute other nuts for the peanuts. Since tahini and sesame butter do not turn into a paste quite so easily, most people prefer to buy them at health foods stores, food cooperatives, or Middle Eastern markets. Nut butters are also available at these same sources.

Usually recipe instructions don't specify whether or not to peel fruits and vegetables. Organically grown produce should not be peeled; a host of nutrients are stored in the skin which also supplies valuable roughage. If you don't know how the food was raised, peel it to avoid eating the wax and pesticides that might be on the skin.

When buying mushrooms, remember that the extremely white ones that show not a trace of dirt have probably been washed in a solution which not only cleans but preserves — chemically. They usually come in cardboard boxes wrapped in cellophane. Buy firm mushrooms with closed gills on the underside. Don't worry about any soil that clings. Do not clean mushrooms until you are ready to use them. Store them in a plastic bag with openings in it so that air can circulate. Just before serving, wipe the mushrooms with a damp paper towel. Cut off a thin slice from the bottom of the stem. Then slice them as you choose.

Lemon juice is an ingredient that appears frequently in raw foods recipes. It contributes flavor and prevents discoloration on those raw fruits and vegetables where the exposed cut surface allows enzymes to react with oxygen. Mushrooms, apples, avocadoes, bananas, peaches, sweet potatoes, and Jerusalem artichokes are some foods that brown quickly. To retain true colors, brush their cut surfaces or toss them with a tablespoon or two of lemon juice.

Squeeze your own lemon juice. Reconstituted brands add sodium bisulfite and sodium benzoate for storage convenience. If it's convenience that you want, take advantage of the bargain prices often advertised for buying lemons in larger quantities. When you feel ambitious, squeeze the juice out of the entire batch and freeze it in ice cube trays in measured quantities of one or two tablespoons. Store the cubes in a sealed container in your freezer, and you'll have a handy supply ready to thaw when needed. You can add zip to juices by serving them on the rocks, add the cubes to a punch bowl, or crush and mix one with salad to keep it crisp and add tang.

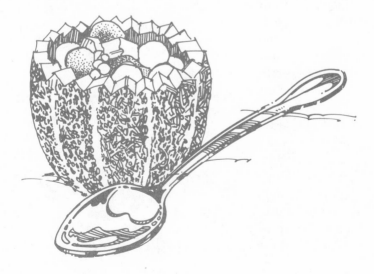

Manner of presentation is important in serving all foods, but perhaps more so for raw foods. They don't give off the strong, luscious aromas that are released when foods are cooked or baked, so appearance must be the first lure. If handled properly, raw foods will exhibit a spectrum of vibrant colors usually dulled in cooking. To capitalize on this quality, wait until just before serving time to get them ready. Allow enough time for molds and frozen items to set and for slaws, marinades, and dressings to develop flavor.

When stuffing tomatoes, peppers, melons, or apples, scallop the edge instead of cutting straight. Take time to consider color combinations of the foods along with the dishware on which you will serve them. Many of the recipes in this book look especially elegant on plain or cut glass.

Garnish, that little decorative extra, can make a world of difference and transform an ordinary, inexpensive dish into regal fare. Serve molds, slaws, cheese mixes, or stuffed fruits and vegetables on a bed or curly dark greens, shredded carrots, or cabbage. Add color and variety in shape and texture with a sprig of parsley, radish roses, sliced or cherry tomatoes, carrot curls, whole berries, or citrus slices. Sprinkle servings with paprika, grated cheese, chopped nuts, coconut, seeds, or greens such as minced chives, dill weed, or parsley.

In spite of inflation and the ever spiraling cost of food, a diet high in raw foods is likely to be more economical than most. The fact that most processed, prepackaged foods will be eliminated from your shopping list will automatically save you many dollars a week. Also, your sources for more direct purchasing like food cooperatives and farmers markets should

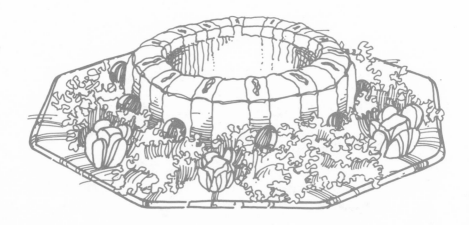

offer lower prices than supermarkets. In addition, certain foods, such as nuts, seeds, and grains, will become staples. You will buy those in quantity through a cooperative or grain mill, and they will certainly be much cheaper than, for example, a box of brown rice from a supermarket.

For fresh items you will have to continue to be a careful shopper, but we assume that your list of sources for comparison will have increased along with your interest in this exciting area of healthful eating.

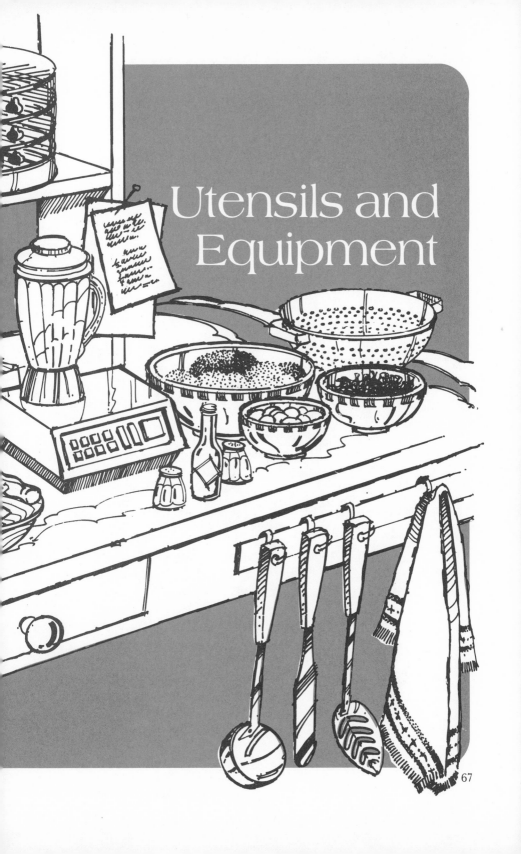

Utensils and
Equipment

**W**hen we eat foods without cooking them, we return to a form of basic living, so it is not surprising that the utensils used to prepare such foods can be simple and few. You can probably make almost any recipe in this book with no more than a fork, spoon, and wire whisk for mixing and beating, glass jars for shaking and blending, spoons and cups for measuring, and knives for cutting, dicing, mincing, and grating. But like specialists in any field, cooks seem to enjoy collecting and using a variety of tools of the trade — sometimes for the timesaving value of the tools, sometimes just for fun.

A sturdy vegetable brush is helpful for cleaning vegetables, especially those root vegetables that retain dirt in their crevices, such as potatoes, Jerusalem artichokes, turnips, and carrots.

Colanders are particularly useful for draining rinsed salad greens and other leafy vegetables. Choose the type with "feet" so that excess water from leaves can drain off.

It is a convenience to have several measuring cups on hand, not just one. If you

are following a recipe that calls for both dry and wet ingredients, you won't have to keep washing your single cup.

Wire mesh strainers of different circumferences and densities come in handy for rinsing grains.

By far the most important tools in any kitchen that means business are good quality cutting knives. With a good 10-inch chef's knife and some practice with the tool, a meal that consists primarily of vegetables will be completed with ease and efficiency; without one, the task will take more time and effort.

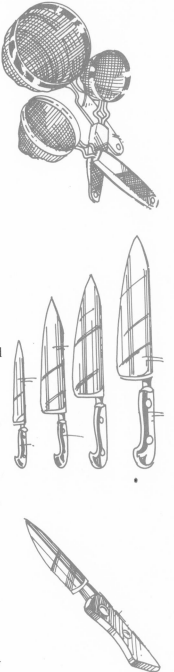

Carbon steel knives are dependable. The edge, although it dulls quickly, always can be sharpened. Unfortunately carbon steel blades tend to rust. The problem can be avoided, however, by drying the knives directly after washing them and rubbing them with oil until they develop a seasoned finish. Stainless steel knives, on the other hand, don't rust and they "hold" an edge longer between sharpenings, but eventually the edge dulls to a point where it cannot be restored. Recently knives with combination carbon steel-stainless steel blades have become available. They seem to offer the advantages of both types of knives — a long-lasting edge that never dulls to ineffectiveness and a nonrusting blade that will not affect the surface of foods. For any of these expect to pay somewhere between $30 and $35 for a 10-inch knife; you will grow to appreciate the investment the more you use your knife.

In addition to a long, heavy knife, you may want a medium-size slicer and a small paring knife. You should also think about buying a good whetstone for sharpening your knife blades. Buy these items from a specialty

shop or department where the salespeople are informed about all the important features of good knives.

The Chinese prefer using cleavers to knives. These are sharp, wide blades attached to a wooden handle. Those who use them frequently contend that the even distribution of weight and the wide cutting surface allow them to chop foods much faster than with conventional knives.

Heavy hardwood, like maple, makes an excellent surface for all the chopping that you will be doing. Culinary shops also feature plastic cutting surfaces which closely resemble marble counter tops. Their price is comparable to wood. One advantage of a small plastic board over a large wooden one is that you can wash it easily in the dishwasher. Thus, traces of garlic, chili peppers, and strong cheeses will be rinsed away with the soapy water.

## The Right Equipment for Chopping and Grinding

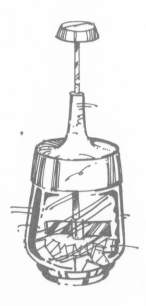

Equipment for grinding or reducing foods is plentiful and varied. Since these techniques are so common to raw foods preparation, having a few selected items will certainly make the job easier.

A "Blitzhacker," a plastic, bell-shaped object with a four-bladed central shaft on a spring, is a good chopper for such foods as onions and nuts. You enclose a portion of food under the bell and bang rhythmically on the handle of the shaft. The choppers chop, rotating as they go, delivering in a very short time a neat portion of minced food.

Graters are tremendous time-savers.

Some are flat steel with different sizes of "teeth"; others are rectangular shaped where each side has a different cutting edge. More elaborate, expensive graters are available. One, a rotary grater, has attachments for different grades of cutting. It is easy to assemble and clean and it is useful for grating large quantities of foods. It costs about $20.

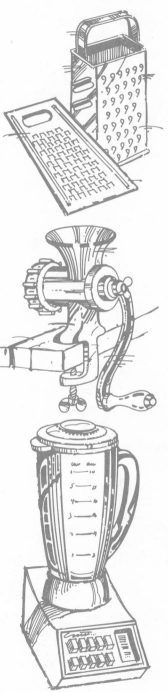

If it is not already part of your collection, you may want to investigate a crank-turned meat grinder, a sturdy piece of kitchen equipment that not only grinds meat but also cheeses, nuts, and soaked grains. Made of strong, heavy iron, it clamps onto the edge of a counter. Depending on which easily assembled disk you use, it grinds a variety of substances into particles ranging from very fine to quite coarse. You can buy one of these new, but as a testimony to their durability, some very old ones still in fine working order appear at garage sales for good prices.

Electric machines are more fallible, but for people whose time for things other than cooking is very precious, their importance is obvious. Anyone who frequently grinds nuts and seeds for drinks and prepared dishes will welcome the convenience a compact coffee grinder provides. A cutting blade in a metal compartment sits on top of a motor encased in plastic. You put a small amount of food in the compartment, cover it with a plastic lid, and push the switch. In seconds you have freshly ground cashews to scatter on cereal or to add to a nutritious fruit drink. A good grinder costs from $25 to $30.

For many years blenders had a corner on the kitchen-machine market. Although you may remember the old, dependable 3-speed blenders, in recent times we've been

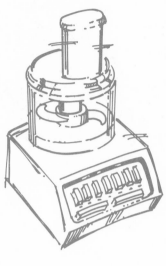

introduced to the 7- and 14-speed ones that "can do anything." Some blenders with strong motors can endure the burden of heavy work, but whether they mince, aerate, or chop with precision is for you to judge. The consensus is that most blenders still do best what they started out doing — blending.

One creative cook, artist, full-time working husband and father we know has transferred his loyalty from a superb collection of Chinese cleavers, handsomely patined wooden cutting bowls and boards to a $250 food processor which "does everything for me," as he puts it. "I get up in the morning, go out and pick vegetables from the garden, and in 10 minutes I have gazpacho to take in a thermos for lunch and enough for dinner as well."

Food processors certainly are the latest big seller in the culinary equipment market. Because of their convenient wide-mouthed bowl and powerful motor and blades, they effectively accomplish all and more of the tasks than the blenders are able to accomplish. If you plan on doing a lot of work in the kitchen but want to limit the time you'll spend there, start looking at processors in department stores and culinary shops. They range in price from $50 to $300. Occasionally culinary shops advertise formal demonstrations which let potential buyers get a feel for the machine before making such a large investment.

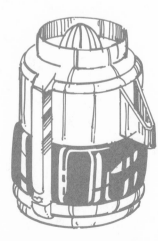

## . . . for Juicing

Since fresh fruit and vegetable juices are high quality, nutritional foods, many people consider a juicer an extremely beneficial investment. Two primary types exist. One,

operating on the principle of centrifugal force,
extracts juice from fruits and vegetables at a
high speed thrust in a spinning basket. The
other "chews" the material under pressure.
Authorities who champion the latter type feel
that it extracts the most enzymes, trace
minerals, and vitamins out of the cells and
fibers of the material.

If you are planning to buy a juicer,
decide what you want it to do for you; find
out if it is easy to use and keep clean, how
efficient it is and how it will fit into your
kitchen in terms of size and color. If you plan
to juice fruits with it, be certain that the
juicer can take a citrus attachment (usually
sold separately). One $200 model offers a
grain-grinding attachment, but none for
citrus. Some juicers are terribly burdensome
to disassemble, clean, and reassemble. Decide
whether you are prepared to go to all that
trouble for a quart of juice.

Of course, price is a consideration.
Expect to pay anywhere from $65 to $700.
Even though you must select according to
your ability to pay, also weigh carefully the
juicer's value to you. Realize that the more
expensive juicers may be offering services you
neither need nor want.

# ... and for Fun

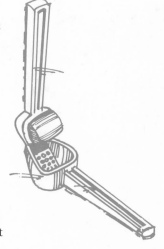

Now here are some more fun objects
from which to pick and choose:

## Garlic Press

Better ones usually imported from
Europe. Metal trap with holes on the bottom
through which crushed garlic appears. Expect
to pay about $5 for a good one.

## Citrus Reamer

Best ones are glass. Many beautiful antique ones exist.

## One-Half Tablespoon Measure

Not a common one but helpful when the recipe calls for that measurement (actually one and one-half teaspoons).

## Melon Baller

For those fancy fruit salads and for butter balls.

## Suribachi

Grooved, Japanese ceramic bowl with wooden pestle for crushing small amounts of fresh herbs and releasing aromatic scents.

## Sprouter

Plastic assembly for sprouting grains, seeds, legumes. Four different trays, each for a different type of sprout.

## Yogurt Maker

Contraption that electrically controls temperatures of fermenting yogurt. Turns out perfect little pots every time. Some have an automatic shutoff switch.

## Pastry Blender

Wires attached to a wooden or plastic handle. Used especially for combining dry ingredients with shortenings or liquids. Nice for making piecrusts and mashing hard-boiled eggs.

## Salad Basket

Wire drying basket with a top that closes over the wet greens.

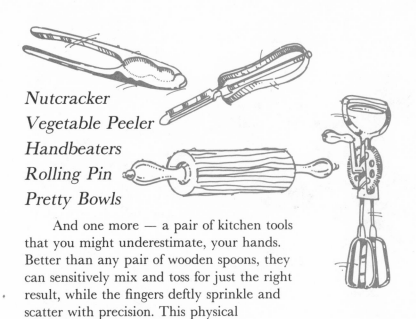

*Nutcracker*
*Vegetable Peeler*
*Handbeaters*
*Rolling Pin*
*Pretty Bowls*

And one more — a pair of kitchen tools that you might underestimate, your hands. Better than any pair of wooden spoons, they can sensitively mix and toss for just the right result, while the fingers deftly sprinkle and scatter with precision. This physical connection with the food is basic to real living.

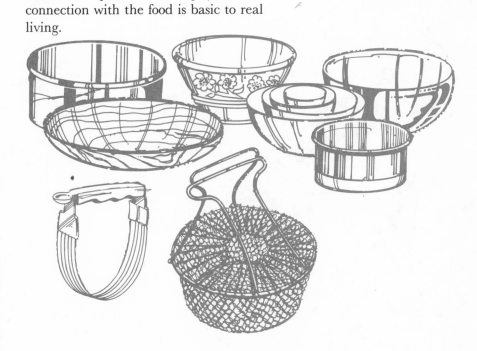

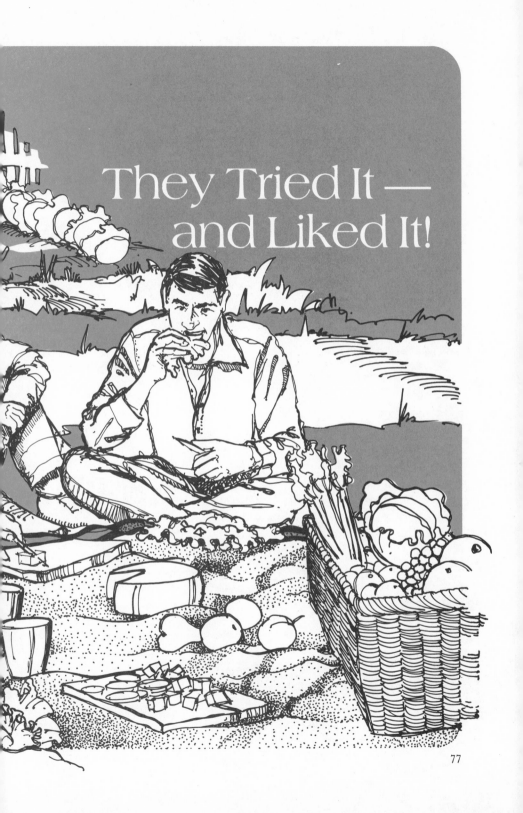

They Tried It —
and Liked It!

$\mathbf{A}$s much as anything we do or say, our food choices reflect our individuality. It is therefore interesting and rewarding to find out how and why certain people increase their intake of raw foods. Perhaps it will help you to make your own decision in the matter.

For some people the value of adding raw foods to the diet is a new discovery, so they start slowly — more salad, more fruit. Others have been enjoying the benefits and satisfactions of eating lots of raw foods for a longer time and they seize every opportunity to renew the pleasure. Some people are "born into" the diet — "My family always ate this way!" — and they are quite comfortable with raw foods. Occasionally a person will come to raw foods unwittingly; for example, a doctor prescribes eating more raw foods and eliminating certain other foods from the diet, and the patient likes the new diet enough to continue it.

One woman we encountered typifies the experience of people just approaching the raw foods idea. She is Sally Barlow, who lives in a fair-size town in northern Pennsylvania. She became conscious of the nutritive value of raw foods when she, like so many others, read the *Organic Gardening*® article about eating the uncooked products of the garden.

## They Were Eating Plenty of Raw Foods Already

"I got to thinking that I ought to eat more raw foods and serve them to my family, too," she says. "So I took a look at our usual menus and was amazed to find how much raw food we were eating already!" She went on to describe what the family usually ate before they stepped up their intake of raw foods.

"My husband, our daughter, and I all began breakfast with fresh fruit or fruit juice. Then my daughter and I usually had cottage cheese and sprouts as a breakfast 'main course.' I commute to work every day, and at midmorning I ate an apple or pear. (In the summer it was a tomato — I'm really mad for vine-ripened tomatoes.)

"Lunch for me would be a cheese or egg sandwich and some raw vegetables. I've always included carrot sticks or green pepper rings or some other kind of raw vegetable when I pack a lunch. The same for the children when they were taking their lunches to school.

"So when I did some reading and learned that enzymes in food are destroyed by cooking, and that we need them, I realized I wouldn't have any trouble adding more raw foods to what my own family was eating — at least in the summer."

Mrs. Barlow said there are several fine farm stands not too far away where she can get fresh produce in season. In addition, the Barlows eat their own organically grown produce as much as possible, although their land is limited in size and all three family members have demanding jobs.

"Our salads grew in size and importance as we made an effort to eat more uncooked foods," Sally continued. "We also ate some delicious, blended, uncooked summer soups.

"Winter is harder, but fortunately there are still salads, and we all are very fond of sprouts. A lot of our winter meals consist of a thick cooked soup, like lentil soup or minestrone, and an enormous salad of fresh greens and grated root vegetables."

Mrs. Barlow knows that a little bit of raw food raises the enzyme level significantly, even if a large part of the meal is cooked. In the winter when she serves cooked beets or other root vegetables, she grates a little of the same vegetable, raw, over it as a garnish. "You can do this with beets, carrots, sweet potatoes, and other root vegetables, and it does add to the taste of your cooked dish.

"We're finding out a lot about the raw foods possibilities that exist," she told us. "There's one farm not too far from here where they grow delicious, tender sweet corn. One day, while I was preparing it for cooking, I thought it looked so good — and I knew it had just been picked — that I tasted it raw. Since then we boil supermarket corn, but we eat farm corn raw. I warm it a bit in our steamer — just enough to melt the butter on it, and we fall to — a regular corn-eating orgy."

She laughed. "Even when I want to, I can't cook vegetables like cauliflower or Brussels sprouts or mushrooms anymore. The family is too quick for me. By the time I get to preparing it, it's been eaten raw — and I'm just as guilty as the others!"

How did the Barlow family take to this eating pattern?

"There was no definite beginning. It just happened," Mrs. Barlow told us. "I was lucky, in that my husband and daughter were ready to eat almost whatever was served to them; neither had that 'How could I possibly eat this?' syndrome. It was just a question of adding more salads, and that pleases my husband enormously. On the rare occasions that, for some reason, there has been no salad at dinner, he says in a despairing tone, 'No salad tonight?' Now I make the salad a main course rather than a side dish more often. From time to time we have a meal featuring fish, meat, or cheese as a raw foods main course.

"We're thriving on it," she said.

## Raw Foods His Key to a New Life

Fran Neilson is a stockmarket investor, a farmer, a businessman, a handwriting analyst, a very good listener, and a rheumatoid arthritic. Now he is also a strong advocate for more raw foods in the diet.

Not long ago Fran was severely crippled, confined to a wheelchair, and barely able to pick up eating utensils or turn his head. Even sitting in his chair caused him serious discomfort.

At a natural-healing clinic Fran was put on a very carefully supervised raw foods diet. He started with several weeks on a liquid fast in which he drank only freshly pressed juices — raw potato, celery, carrot, and combination vegetable juices. He also drank a vegetable broth made from powdered vegetables diluted in warm water. Gradually his diet was expanded to include specific fruit juices and raw vegetable salads and fruit salads — as much as he could eat. As Fran's body started showing small signs of improvement, the doctors added more variety and protein.

At breakfast he would eat soaked raw millet with goat's milk and some fresh fruit. Fran's lunches included raw grated potatoes, a large vegetable salad, lots of sprouts, especially alfalfa, goat milk cheese, and sometimes a slice of 100 percent rye bread.

Soon Fran was progressing noticeably. Within several weeks his diet became much broader, although the basic foods with which he started still were most important, and he did continue to drink the fresh juices.

After less than three months of treatment, Fran was walking with a cane. A year later he visited his brother in Arizona. He drove there from Wisconsin. For Fran Neilson a diet rich in raw foods turned out to be the key to a new and productive life.

# Family Thrives on Diet of Over 50 Percent Raw Foods

Two years ago Stephanie Shefrin didn't have enough energy to stay awake beyond 4:30 or 5:00 p.m. each day. A young divorced woman working in the fast-paced merchandising industry, she had begun to experience really severe dizziness, depression, and fatigue. "Previous to these days," she told us, "I did a good deal of social drinking, ate quick prepared foods, sometimes pizza with the girls or steak and potatoes with a date on nights out. I drank lots and lots of coffee to keep going. I barely had the strength to take care of my two children, then four and six."

During this time Stephanie met Dr. David Shefrin who is now her husband. He diagnosed Stephanie as a diabetic and encouraged her to try the regenerative diet program that he had been using successfully with his patients.

Soon, while also adhering to specific guidelines for her diabetic condition, Stephanie and her family began to follow a food program that included at least 50 to 75 percent raw foods: an abundance of raw fruits, vegetables, and sprouts accompanied by a high quantity of low-fat cottage cheese as a good protein source.

They have replaced caffeine, sweeteners, and most alcoholic beverages with herb teas and warm water with lemon. The remainder of the diet consists of carefully chosen and prepared fish, lightly cooked, a very small amount of cooked meat, lightly steamed vegetables, some cooked grains and beans, and an occasional baked, unsweetened dessert.

We asked if meal planning and shopping are more difficult when a family eats this way. "Not at all," Stephanie replied. "Actually planning and shopping are no longer chores. With this much simpler diet, there are fewer items to buy. We find a good source for unsprayed fruits and vegetables, shop for grains and beans at a natural foods store, and seek a reliable person or store where we can buy untreated meat and fresh fish. Since we very consciously attempt to eliminate cholesterol from the diet, we do not need to shop for foods that once were almost staples in more elaborate meals. Oils of all kinds, butter, full-fat creams, and eggs (usually) are off the shopping list."

Stephanie reiterated what so many other people who use a large percentage of raw foods have told us. "We spend much less time planning and buying, but best of all, we spend less time cleaning up. That means more time for other things."

Stephanie says that the aches and pains that plagued her have virtually disappeared, along with her depressions and fatigue. She feels in charge of her life once more.

The family is so involved in shopping for, preparing, and eating the eye-appealing, tasteful dishes that new traditions are forming. Tabletime discussions regarding the value for such foods is common. "As a matter of fact," says Stephanie, "the children actually look around in restaurants and notice that 'the man at that table is eating food that will not keep him healthy.' "

The family chooses restaurants that serve a buffet so that they can balance the raw with the cooked foods and skip the sauces and all other foods that do not fit into their diet.

When the Shefrins invite friends for dinner or take a covered dish to another home, they prepare their usual fare. Stephanie's no-bake cheesecake is always a hit. Most tasters like it better than the rich baked variety. As they share such dishes and ideas with others, the Shefrins find that more and more people want to try eating in a similar fashion.

# Old-Fashioned Cook
# Slips Easily into the Raw Foods Routine

The experience of Amanda Nancoff is similar. "My background is German and Hungarian," she told us. "Both of my grandmothers were professional cooks and bakers in Europe and then they continued in that activity for a very large part of every day at home after they immigrated into this country.

"An only child, I grew up close to my working mother. I learned to cook at an early age; at 11 I was preparing complete meals — mainly roasted meats, potatoes, vegetables, and salads. I loved desserts, so I started making them too."

Now Amanda is a working mother herself, teaching French full time during the school year. We met her while she was conducting a 10-week evening cooking course in natural foods. Her course ran the gamut — bread baking, vegetarian main dishes, healthful snacks and desserts, soups, beverages, sandwiches, information on shopping, and instruction on how to use grains, legumes, and sprouts.

Upon getting to know her a little better and visiting back and forth in the summer, we were surprised to discover that Amanda and her family rarely ate the kind of cooked dishes that she demonstrated in her classes. In the early morning she had her freshly squeezed vegetable or fruit juice and went out to work in her garden for at least an hour. Then into the house for a breakfast of raw fruits, nuts, seeds, and herb tea or a big bowl of muesli, yogurt, and a warm grain beverage. Other mornings she might pick a few scallions, radishes, green beans, cherry tomatoes, some lettuce, and a big green pepper and eat them with scoops of home-made cottage cheese and thin slices of homemade whole-grain bread and butter. As a beverage Amanda often prepared a juice made from a wide assortment of vegetables, including tomatoes, onions, cabbage, parsley, and herbs.

At lunchtime, when she was free for a nice visit in the sun, she frequently invited friends to share her bounty. The table at one of these lunches would encompass lots of garden vegetables, a big block of raw milk cheese, a jar of peanut or other nut butter, a delicious spread made from mashed tofu, tahini, vegetables, and herbs to be wrapped in leaves of red Swiss chard or spinach. An earthenware crock held a pitcher of cold herb tea garnished with lemon rings and fresh mint — and in the center of the table, slices of warm herb bread.

## The Best and the Freshest Foods Available

Some of Amanda's dishes that we particularly enjoyed were a cold fruit soup made from fruit juice, fresh fruit, nuts, yogurt, and sweet spices; a stuffed zucchini filled with a vegetable cottage cheese; and a raw vegetable-nut loaf with a tahini sauce.

Of course we asked the obvious question, "Why all the raw foods?"

"They're available — the best that I can grow and the freshest that I can ever get them. They're also the most nutritious this way. And why spend any part of a glorious summer day inside when you can be outside? This kind of food preparation allows me more time to pursue other interests. When the winter comes, it's back to more cooked foods, dried grains and beans, warm soups, and extensive bread baking."

Amanda told us that she shopped every place she could find an interesting variety of good food and good prices. Some of her favorite haunts were the produce and cheese stands at the country farmers market, grain mills that sell both retail and wholesale, food cooperatives for bulk items, raw milk dairies, and local farms where she bought eggs. She also had a long list of "connections," people who provided specialties like homemade cheeses and ethnic breads.

"We've been eating natural foods in my family for many years," she told us. "My husband is already well accustomed to a nice balance between raw and cooked foods. When summer arrives and the balance shifts quite a bit, he says it is a welcome change.

"My daughter, on the other hand, is not 100 percent sold on the way that we eat. She feels a lot of pressure from other 10-year-olds in school who examine the lunches she brings and generally classify them as 'odd.' " Nonetheless, it is this child who created the sweetened yogurt dessert that was one of the highlights of Amanda's cooking course. Also, Amanda told us, her daughter could eat raw vegetables, sprouts, cottage cheese, and whole-grain bread almost exclusively. "The other day when I came home, she was making tacos with chopped, raw vegetables, shredded cheeses, and yogurt — all on a warm corn tortilla."

# MONDAY

## Morning

Breakfast Dip served with sliced fresh fruits
Celestial Shake

## Afternoon

Summer Stuffed Peppers
Hearts of Celery
Salad Greens with Blue Cheese Dressing
Lemon-Limeade

## Evening

Cottage Cheese ... Strawberry Dressing

# A Week's Worth of Marvelous Raw Foods Menus

**P**erhaps you are unaccustomed to fish for breakfast, or to making an entire meal of mostly fruit foods; maybe you don't feel satisfied without a dessert at the end of your dinner. Of course you know you're not alone. But we urge you to try these unusual ideas. At the same time, let the special appeal of raw foods work its magic on you. Try a few of the menus just as they are. You can always go back to old eating habits if you like. But we doubt that you will!

Here you will find carefully selected combinations of foods for maximum nutrition and flavor. Each meal contains the complete protein you need even if it contains no meat, fish, or cheese.

You will note that the noon meal is the big meal of the day. For most efficient use of food by the body, nutritionists suggest that the largest meal be taken in the afternoon, before most people have completed the day's work. We also include a choice of snacks, in case you prefer eating lightly throughout the day instead of taking three full meals.

# Day 1

## Morning

Breakfast Dip* served with sliced fresh fruits *pg 102*
Celestial Shake*  *104*

## Afternoon

Summer Stuffed Peppers*  *190*
Hearts of Celery*  *237*
Salad greens with Blue Cheese Dressing*  *163*
Lemon-Limeade*  *116*

## Evening

Bowl of cottage cheese
Fresh fruit chunks with Strawberry Dressing*  *168*
Blueberry Bread*  *268*
Apple and Orange Smoothie*  *111*

## Snack

Peanut and Banana Soup*  *141*
Carrot and Almond Bars*  *269*

*See Index for recipe.

# Day 2

## Morning

Cucumbers Stuffed with Salmon*
Pepper and Carrot Juice*

## Afternoon

Assorted Cheesy Bites*
Vegetable Marvel Loaf*
Artichokes and Flowers*
Chopped cabbage with Sour Cream Dressing*
Cucumber and Yogurt Drink*

## Evening

Crunchy Peanut Butter Spread* on zucchini disks
Gelled Blue Cheese and Green Vegetables*
Salad Relish*
Tomato Juice*

## Snack

Coconut and Pineapple Goody*
Apple Delight*

*See Index for recipe.

# Day 3

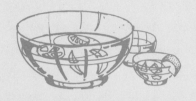

## Morning

Oats and Cheese with Fruit*
Comfrey Drink*

## Afternoon

Sun-Kissed Vegetable Soup*
Stuffed Veal and Almond Rolls*
Green salad with French Housewife's Shallot
    Dressing*
Gardener's Sun Punch*

## Evening

Gazpacho*
Grain Salad with Parsley Sauce*
Celery stalks filled with Cottage Dip*
Springwater served with slices of lemon
    and a mint sprig

## Snack

Summer Refresher*
Grape Ice Cream*

*See Index for recipe.

# Day 4

## Morning

A.M. Salad with Yogurt*
Cold Spiced Cider*

## Afternoon

Crunchy Tomato Soup*
Curried Rye and Tofu*
Shredded mixed vegetables with Table Mountain
    Dressing*
Cucumber and Yogurt Drink*

## Evening

Summer Seas Soup*
Buckwheat Groats Salad*
Carrot Top and Garlic Pie Filling* in crust

## Snack

Vanilla Limeade*
Grapefruit Cup*

*See Index for recipe.

# Day 5

## Morning

Energy Glow Breakfast*
Honeydew Cocktail*

## Afternoon

Cool Green Soup*
Swordfish Shish with Dill Dressing*
Watercress Salad*
Coeur a la Creme*

## Evening

Raw Spinach with Mushrooms*
Tofu Alfalfa Slaw with Apples*
Gardener's Sun Punch*

## Snack

Fruit Slices*
Pecan-Roquefort Hors d'Oeuvres*

*See Index for recipe.

# Day 6

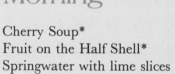

## Morning

Cherry Soup*
Fruit on the Half Shell*
Springwater with lime slices

## Afternoon

Marinated Fish Tahitian Style*
Lettuce with Sesame Seeds*
Goober Slaw*
Sunbaked Fruit Bread*

## Evening

Assorted sandwich tray, including the following:
Banana Bread* with Cranberry Relish*
Apple slices with Cinnamon-Honey Spread*
Green tomato slices with Golden Sandwich Filling*
Provolone cheese slices
   with Avocado Sandwich Filling*
Carrot-Celery Juice*

## Snack

Kefir Conglomeration*
Nutty Fruit Tarts*

*See Index for recipe.

# Day 7

## Morning

Ceviche*
Turnip Slaw*
Homemade Kefir* garnished
  with minced green onions

## Afternoon

Lettuce Rolls*
Avocadoes and Mushrooms Cosmopolitan*
Fresh Carrot Chutney*
Springwater served over Frozen Flower Fancy*

## Evening

Cold Zuke Soup*
Vegetarian Liver Pate* with Cucumber Dip*
Beet Salad*

## Snack

Raw vegetable tray served with Labneh Dip*
Banana Split Stick*

*See Index for recipe.

# The Recipes

## Salt

The recipes in this book do not list salt as an ingredient. There is strong evidence that salt is a factor in the incidence of circulatory problems and other common ailments, so its use is not recommended.

Of course, it's up to you to decide how your food will be seasoned — with herbs, spices, or even salt. But we think you'll be surprised at how good these foods taste without salt. We urge you to try them that way first.

# part two

# Breakfast

# Breakfast

2½ cups wheat sprouts      3 sliced bananas
¾ cup sunflower seeds      ½ cup raisins
¼ cup sesame seeds      ½ cup plain yogurt
3 grated apples with skin

# A.M. Salad with Yogurt

Mix ingredients in a large bowl.

**Yield: 6 servings**

---

1 quart raw or pasteurized      2-3 tablespoons yogurt
milk      starter

# Homemade Yogurt

Pour milk into a saucepan (avoid aluminum) and heat to about 110°F. With a wire whisk, blend in room temperature yogurt starter (saved from a previous batch of yogurt or "plain" yogurt from a store). Pour into a wide-mouth glass jar and cover. (Make certain that liquid does not come into contact with metal lid.)

Place in an area that maintains a steady temperature between 105° and 110°F. Gas ovens with pilot lights, heating pads, and electric skillets filled with a little water, closets with exposed heat pipes, shelves directly over a radiator are all possible places for incubation. You may have to wrap the jar in tea towels in order to maintain the temperature.

Freshness of milk, starter, and temperature are all factors that will affect the incubating time. Yogurt will be "set up" anywhere between 3 and 8 hours. To check the yogurt, very gently tip the jars. If the mixture resembles a moderately thick custard, it is complete.*

*About ¾ cup dry milk solids whisked into the milk before heating will produce a firmer yogurt that more closely resembles sour cream in consistency.*

[continued on next page]

Refrigerate until well chilled. (The yogurt will appear firmer after refrigeration.)

Before using, pour off the watery liquid (whey) that might appear on top. Add any flavorings now, not during the culturing process as the results are often uneven.

*Yield: 1 quart*

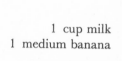

1 cup milk
1 medium banana

1-2 tablespoons peanut butter

## Blender Breakfast

Process ingredients in an electric blender to liquefy.

*Yield: 1 serving*

2 cups peanut butter
½ cup sesame seeds

¼ teaspoon Homemade Vanilla Extract (see recipe below)

## Breakfast Dip

Combine ingredients. Mix well.
Serve with sliced fruit.

*Yield: 2½ cups*

2 vanilla beans
½ cup boiling water
1 teaspoon liquid lecithin

2 tablespoons honey
2 tablespoons oil

## Homemade Vanilla Extract

Cut vanilla beans into small pieces and place them in a bowl. Pour boiling water over them, cover the bowl, and allow mixture to steep overnight.

Grind mixture in an electric blender. Strain and return juice to the blender. Add lecithin, honey, and oil. Blend mixture and pour into a bottle. Cap tightly and store in the refrigerator.

Shake liquid well before using. Measure the same amount as any commercial vanilla extract when you use your favorite recipe.

*Yield: about ¾ cup*

---

¾ cup oat sprouts
⅓ cup pumpkin seeds
⅓ cup raisins
1 grated apple with skin

1 sliced banana
¼ cup cottage cheese, blended

## Breakfast Salad

Combine ingredients. Toss lightly.

*Yield: 6   ½-cup servings*

2 cups milk
1 teaspoon carob powder
1 tablespoon almond butter
2 tablespoons honey

1 teaspoon brewer's yeast
1 teaspoon kelp powder
½ cup alfalfa sprouts
(optional)

## Celestial Shake

Combine ingredients in an electric blender, set speed for frappe, and process until smooth.

Serve at breakfast time or as a quick pick-me-up between meals.

**Yield: 2 servings**

*Variation: Fruit may be substituted for the carob if desired.*

---

¼ cup raisins
½ cup diced apples
½ cup diced peaches
½ cup diced bananas
¼ cup pitted dates

2 tablespoons sunflower
  seeds
2 tablespoons sesame seeds
wheat germ
milk

## Energy Glow Breakfast

Mix fruits and seeds in a medium-size bowl. Sprinkle wheat germ over all.

Add milk to moisten. Let sit a few minutes before serving.

**Yield: 4 servings**

1 cup millet (see Index)   ½ cup chopped sunflower
2 tablespoons flax seeds      seeds
                    water   2 sliced pears
2 tablespoons chopped   1 teaspoon honey
          pecans

## Grain, Nuts, and Seeds with Fruit

Grind millet and flax seeds and soak in water to cover overnight. In the morning add pecans, sunflower seeds, and pears. Mix with honey and serve.

**Yield: 2 servings**

---

2 cups sunflower seeds   1 cup almonds
1 cup pumpkin seeds   ⅓ cup sifted carob powder

## High Protein Cereal

Grind sunflower seeds, pumpkin seeds, and almonds in a nut grinder.
Add carob powder and mix thoroughly.
Serve with fruit juice, milk, or fruit.

**Yield: 4 cups**

---

1 banana   1 cup chilled apple juice
1 egg

## Nature's Instant Breakfast

Process ingredients for a few seconds in an electric blender.

**Yield: 1 serving**

*Variation: Flavor can be varied by blending apple juice 50-50 with another juice (such as grape, cranberry, or prune).*

6 cups rolled oats   2 cups plain yogurt
4 cups apple juice   2 cups cottage cheese
½ cup almonds   3 cups berries

## Oats and Cheese with Fruit

Soak oats in apple juice 30 minutes.

Process almonds in an electric blender until coarsely chopped. Add yogurt and cottage cheese and process until well mixed.

Divide oats among 6 bowls and top each with a serving of cheese mixture. Sprinkle ½ cup berries over each portion. Serve immediately.

*Yield: 6 servings*

---

½ cup wheat germ   1 teaspoon honey or to
1 teaspoon sesame seeds   taste
1 sliced banana   milk to taste

## Simple Breakfast Cereal

Pour wheat germ into a cereal bowl. Sprinkle with sesame seeds. Add banana.

Sweeten to taste with honey. Serve with milk.

*Yield: 1 serving*

---

2 cups sunflower sprouts
1 cored apple (peel only if skin is tough)
2 tablespoons pineapple juice

½ cubed honeydew melon
1 cup combined crushed pineapple and pitted dark sweet cherries

## Sunflower Pudding

Process ingredients in an electric blender until smooth. Serve chilled.

*Yield: 6 servings*

6 cups rolled oats          2 cups orange juice
¾ cup raisins              1 cup water
¾ cup chopped dried        1½ cups shredded coconut
  apricots                 1 cup heavy cream

## Tropical Oats

Soak oats, raisins, and apricots in the combined orange juice and water; cover at room temperature at least 1 hour.

Stir mixture and divide equally among 6 bowls. Sprinkle ¼ cup coconut over each portion.

Beat cream until it stands in loose peaks (do not overbeat).

Top each serving with a dollop of whipped cream and serve immediately.

**Yield: 6 servings**

# Beverages

# Beverages

¾ cup apple juice    1 tablespoon lemon juice
¾ cup orange juice   1½ teaspoons sour cream

## Apple and Orange Smoothie

Process ingredients in an electric blender until smooth.

**Yield: 1½ cups**

---

3 cups milk    1 tablespoon carob powder
1 teaspoon honey   ½ banana

## Carob-Banana Milk

Process ingredients in an electric blender until smooth.

**Yield: 3 cups**

---

¾ pound carrots    4 celery stalks

## Carrot-Celery Juice
## from a Juicer

Cut off carrot tops about ¼ inch to eliminate any hidden dirt. Scrub carrots with a strong vegetable brush. Cut them lengthwise only if they are too large to fit into the feeder throat of the juicer.

Separate the celery bunch and wash the stalks. Cut each stalk in half.

Feed vegetables into feeder throat of juicer at a steady medium speed. Use the plastic or wooden tamper to help push the vegetables

[continued on next page]

through and to ensure that you do not harm your fingers.

Follow instructions that accompany juicer for setting up, disassembling, and cleaning the machine.

*Yield: about 1 pint*

| 1 quart apple cider | 12 whole cloves |
| ½ cup honey | ⅛ teaspoon nutmeg |
| 6 lemon slices | 6 cinnamon sticks |

## Cold Spiced Cider

Combine all ingredients but cinnamon sticks; let stand 1 hour. Strain.

Pour into 6 mugs. Add cinnamon stick to each mug for stirring.

*Yield: 6   ¾-cup servings*

| 4 cups apple juice | 3-4 mint sprigs |
| 5 medium comfrey leaves | 2 bananas |

## Comfrey Drink

Process ingredients in an electric blender for a minute or so, or until the comfrey is well liquefied.

Strain into glasses. Serve immediately.

*Yield: 6 servings*

1½ cups plain yogurt or      1 tablespoon chopped green
      kefir (see Index)             onions
   3 peeled cucumbers

## Cucumber and Yogurt Drink

Process ingredients in an electric blender until smooth.
Chill well before serving.

**Yield: 6 servings**

2 peeled, chunked              ½ avocado
      cucumbers               ½ juiced lemon or lime

## Cuke Cooler

Process ingredients in an electric blender until well liquefied.

**Yield: 3-4 servings**

1 cup plain yogurt     12 pitted dates or to taste
   1 cup milk           4 ground almonds
   4 ice cubes

## Date Shake

Process ingredients thoroughly in an electric blender.
Chill and serve.

**Yield: 3 cups**

|                          |                       |
|-------------------------:|-----------------------|
| mint leaves             | 1 crushed nutmeg      |
| lemon balm leaves       | 6 whole cloves        |
| bergamot leaves         | 8-10 crushed rose hips |
| comfrey leaves          | hot water             |
| 3 cinnamon sticks, broken | 1 sliced orange     |
| into pieces             | 1 sliced lemon        |
| 4 pods coriander seeds  |                       |

# Gardener's Sun Punch

On a sunny day fill a wide-mouth gallon jar with leaves, cinnamon sticks, seeds, nutmeg, cloves, and rose hips. Cover with water. Allow to sit in full sun 3 hours. During last hour, add orange and lemon slices.

Finally, strain liquid. Return fruit slices to it and refrigerate until serving time.

**Yield: about 1 gallon**

---

about ¾ cup kefir grains*    1 quart raw or pasteurized milk

# Homemade Kefir

In a clean glass jar, pour milk over kefir grains. Cover and allow liquid to remain at room temperature several days until the milk has thickened to a junketlike consistency.

Pour it through a sieve. Refrigerate the kefir liquid.

Rinse kefir grains in cool water and start a new batch of kefir, or cover them with water and refrigerate them no longer than a week. Eventually you will have more grains than you will need for a quart of liquid. At this point, consider using kefir more frequently or start sharing these jewels with friends.

**Yield: 1 quart**

*Active kefir grains, the fermenting agents, may be ordered from R-A-J Biological Laboratory, 35 Park Avenue, Blue Point, NY 11715.*

1 quart raw or pasteurized   2-3 tablespoons piima
milk        culture*

# Homemade Piima

With a wire whisk, blend the piima culture with milk. Pour into a wide-mouth glass jar, cover, and allow to set at room temperature 8-24 hours until the milk has reached a slightly thickened consistency.

Refrigerate. Save a few tablespoons as a starter for the next batch.

Piima is milder than both kefir or yogurt. Without hesitation, you can use it in recipes in place of milk.

**Yield: 1 quart**

*Freeze-dried piima culture may be obtained from PIIMA, Box 2614, La Mesa, CA 92041.*

---

3 cups orange juice   3 teaspoons lemon juice
3 cups diced honeydew or
cantaloupe

# Honeydew Cocktail

Process ingredients in an electric blender until well liquefied.
Serve chilled.

**Yield: 6 servings**

---

3 cups milk   freshly ground nutmeg for
4 eggs        garnish
3 tablespoons honey

# Honey Eggnog

Process milk, eggs, and honey in an electric blender until smooth.
Garnish with nutmeg.

**Yield: 3½ cups**

16 ounces kefir (see Index)
2 juiced oranges
1 juiced lime
1 grated orange rind
1 banana

6 ice cubes
2 tablespoons wheat germ
2 teaspoons pure vanilla extract
3 tablespoons honey or to taste

## Kefir Conglomeration

Combine ingredients and blend until ice cubes have broken up and drink is thick and frothy.

**Yield: about 3 cups**

---

4 tablespoons honey or to taste
1 cup hot water
3 cups water
3 juiced lemons

3 juiced limes
whole rind ½ lemon and ½ lime
mint sprigs

## Lemon-Limeade

Whir honey and hot water in an electric blender until honey is dissolved. Add rest of water, juices, and rinds.

Refrigerate until well chilled. Remove rinds.

Serve over crushed ice with mint sprigs.

**Yield: about 5 cups**

---

2 cups milk
1 teaspoon honey
1 tablespoon tahini

½ cup wheat germ or rolled oats
1 egg (optional)

## Long-Distance Runner's Energy Smoothie

Process ingredients in an electric blender until smooth.

**Yield: 2 servings**

1 cup milk   1 heaping tablespoon
1 cup plain yogurt      peanut butter
1 banana

## Monkey Shake

Combine ingredients in the order listed in an electric blender. Process for several seconds or until mixture is well blended.

**Yield: 2 servings**

---

¼ cup ground cashews   3 sliced bananas
1 cup milk   ¼ teaspoon kelp

## Nut Milk Shake

Liquefy cashews and milk in an electric blender. Add remaining ingredients and process until smooth.

Serve immediately.

**Yield: 2 servings**

---

1 tablespoon honey
½ cup warm water        1 peeled lemon
3 peeled oranges        1 cup ice cubes

## Orangeade

Dissolve honey in water.

Process in an electric blender with fruits until liquefied. Add ice and process until ice is finely chopped.

Serve at once.

**Yield: 3 cups**

¼ cup parsley    2 tablespoons cream
¼ cup grated carrots

# Parsley Juice

Process ingredients in an electric blender until smooth.
This is also very good as a sauce for vegetables.

*Yield: 2   ¼-cup (2-ounce) servings*

---

6 tablespoons peanut butter
6 cups milk                    ¼ teaspoon pure vanilla
3 teaspoons honey              extract

# Peanut Butter Milk

Combine ingredients and beat smooth.

*Yield: 6 servings*

---

8 chopped carrots    4 chopped green peppers

# Pepper and Carrot Juice

Process ingredients in an electric blender.
Chill before serving.

*Yield: 6 servings*

*Note: This is a thick beverage, rich in vitamins and minerals. Because of its pulpy consistency, it should be eaten slowly, with a spoon. As an alternative, add enough water to make a beverage consistency and strain.*

4 separated eggs
2 cups piima (see Index)
1 tablespoon ground
   almonds

1 teaspoon pure vanilla
   extract
4 tablespoons honey
few pinches freshly grated
   nutmeg

# Piima Eggnog

Blend all ingredients but egg whites and nutmeg.
Whip egg whites separately. Fold into blended mixture.
Serve immediately in chilled punch glasses. Garnish with nutmeg.

*Yield: 3½ cups*

---

1 chunked pineapple
½ cup coconut chunks
milk from inside coconut

1½ juiced oranges or
   enough to sweeten to taste
1 cup ice cubes

# Pina-Colada

Process pineapple in an electric blender to liquefy. Add coconut, coconut milk, and orange juice. Process until smooth. Add ice and process until finely chopped.

*Yield: 3 cups*

---

1 cup chunked pineapple
½ cup pineapple juice
3 chopped carrots

¼ peeled lemon
1 cup ice cubes

# Pineapple-Carrot Juice

Process pineapple, juice, carrots, and lemon in an electric blender until smooth. Add ice cubes and process until finely chopped.
Serve at once.

*Yield: 2 cups*

8 radishes   1 small parsley sprig
1 tablespoon light cream   ¼ teaspoon rosemary

# Radish Cocktail

Process ingredients in an electric blender until smooth.

**Yield: ½ cup**

---

3 stalks rhubarb (remove
leaves as they are toxic)   ¼ peeled lemon
1 cup apple juice   1 teaspoon honey

# Rhubarb-Apple Juice

Process ingredients in an electric blender until smooth.

**Yield: 2 cups**

*Note: Rhubarb juice should be consumed sparingly and in combination with other juices because it is high in oxalic acid, which is undesirable in high concentrations.*

---

1 cup plain yogurt   1 teaspoon honey or to taste
2 cups raspberries (or other berries)

# Summer Refresher

Process ingredients in an electric blender until smooth and serve in tall stemmed glasses.

**Yield: 3 servings**

1½ cups sunflower seeds   3 tablespoons honey or to taste
3 cups warm water   milk or orange juice to thin
3 bananas   if desired

## Sunflower Shake

Soak sunflower seeds in water overnight.

In the morning process seeds and water in an electric blender. Add bananas and honey and process until smooth. If the mixture is too thick, add more water, milk, or orange juice to reach desired consistency.

**Yield: 6 servings**

---

3 cups (6 tomatoes) tomato juice   1 stalk celery with leaves
1 tablespoon green pepper juice   1 tablespoon lemon juice
1 parsley sprig   freshly ground horseradish
1 green onion

## Tomato Juice

Process all ingredients except horseradish in an electric blender until liquefied.

Season to taste with horseradish before serving.

**Yield: 3 cups**

---

1 cup diced tomatoes   1 teaspoon chopped onion
2 cups milk   or dash onion juice
1 tablespoon lemon juice   dash Tabasco

## Tomato Juice Appetizer

Process ingredients in an electric blender until smooth.

**Yield: 4   ¾-cup servings**

3 cups plain yogurt
1 cup chilled lime juice
honey to taste

grated vanilla bean for
garnish

## Vanilla Limeade

Process yogurt, lime juice, and honey in an electric blender until smooth. Pour into chilled glasses.

Grate a bit of vanilla bean on each serving.

*Yield: 6 servings*

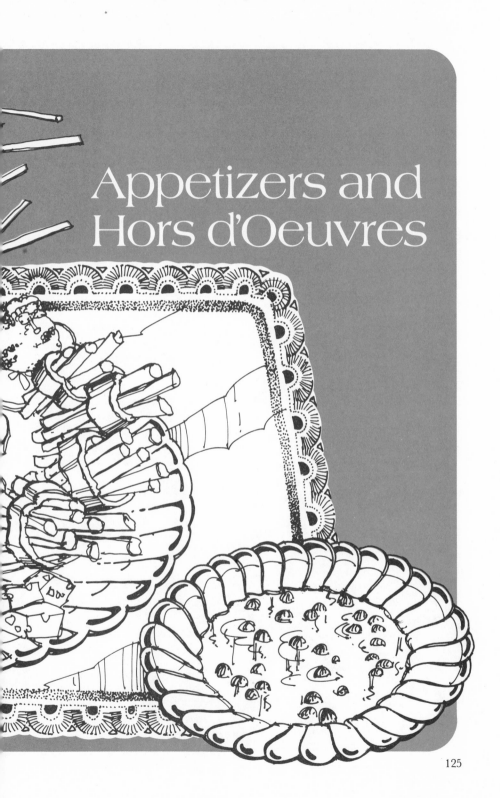

# Appetizers and
# Hors d'Oeuvres

# Appetizers and Hors d'Oeuvres

Zucchini Tartares              Mushrooms Stuffed with Almonds
Green Bean Bundles            Chrysanthemums

## Antipasto Plate

Divide Zucchini Tartares, Green Bean Bundles, Mushrooms Stuffed with Almonds, and Chrysanthemums into equal portions and serve as main course.

**Yield: 6 servings**

---

½ pound Beef Tartare (see    1 ½-inch-sliced zucchini
Index)                        parsley for garnish

## Zucchini Tartares

Roll Beef Tartare into meatballs. Place each ball on a zucchini slice, pressing it down slightly.

Using tweezers, press a small parsley sprig into the center of each ball.

---

½ pound young green          2 small ¼-inch-sliced sweet
beans                         red peppers

## Green Bean Bundles

Place several green beans in the center of each pepper round; set on end so that beans fit snugly. If there are any extra rings, just slip them on the completed bean bundles.

8 large mushrooms, stems
    removed and reserved
½ cup ground almonds

2 tablespoons plain yogurt
1 teaspoon chopped dill
½ teaspoon tamari soy sauce

## Mushrooms Stuffed with Almonds

Mince mushroom stems and mix almonds, yogurt, dill, and soy sauce. Mound mixture into mushroom caps.

---

4 peeled young turnips    4 peeled young beets

## Chrysanthemums

Place a vegetable in the bowl of a wooden spoon. Using a very sharp knife, cut vegetable into thin rows from one end to the other. The bowl of the wooden spoon will stop the knife so that it does not cut through to the bottom of the vegetable. Rotate vegetable a quarter turn and slice across the previous cuts, again not quite through to the bottom.

Place in a bowl of ice water for 30 minutes or longer, which will cause the petals to open slightly. Before serving, pat dry with a paper towel.

---

1 cup dry cottage cheese,
    sieved
¼ cup plain yogurt
1 cup finely chopped
    peanuts, pecans, or
    walnuts

1 teaspoon tamari soy sauce
chopped parsley, chopped
    chives, sesame seeds, or
    any ground nuts

## Assorted Cheesy Bites

Combine first 4 ingredients and blend well. Chill until firm.
Shape spoonfuls of mixture into 1-inch logs or balls. Roll in parsley,

chives, sesame seeds, or nuts.

Refrigerate until ready to serve.

**Yield: 36 hors d'oeuvres**

*Note: The mixture may be somewhat sticky, so it is a good idea to butter your hands before forming the logs or balls.*

## Carrot Curls

With carrots at room temperature, cut long, very thin slices with a vegetable peeler. Roll each slice into a circle and insert a threaded needle through carrot, slipping it onto the thread. Continue until you have a long string of curls, and place them in ice water. Chill for 1 hour.

When you are ready to add the curls to your salad, clip thread and gently slip carrots off.

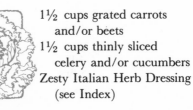

|  |  |
|---|---|
| 6 large lettuce leaves | 1½ cups grated carrots |
| 3 cups sprouts (alfalfa or mixture) | and/or beets |
| 3 tablespoons finely chopped green peppers, onions, or chives | 1½ cups thinly sliced celery and/or cucumbers |
|  | Zesty Italian Herb Dressing (see Index) |

## Lettuce Leaf Crepes

Toss vegetables lightly and place on lettuce leaves. Drizzle with dressing. Roll as for crepes.

**Yield: 6 servings**

18 large mushroom caps      1 tablespoon grated onions
1 cup (4 ounces) spinach    1 minced garlic clove
1 cup cottage cheese        1 teaspoon dill
(blended) or sour cream

## Mushroom Caps Florentine

Wash mushroom caps and set aside.

Process spinach in an electric blender about ¼ cup at a time or chop it finely with a sharp knife.

In a small bowl, mix together cottage cheese, onions, garlic, and dill.

In a medium-size bowl, combine spinach and cottage cheese, mixing thoroughly.

Fill caps with spinach and chill well before serving.

*Yield: 18 pieces*

½ pound Roquefort cheese
¼ cup butter                    dash tamari soy sauce
1 teaspoon grated onions        pinch pepper
⅛ cup minced celery             48 pecan halves

## Pecan-Roquefort Hors d'Oeuvres

Mash all ingredients but nuts. Beat until smooth and well blended. Chill until hardened.

With moistened hands, roll mixture into 1-inch-diameter balls. Press 2 pecan halves on either side of each cheese ball. Chill until ready to serve or serve immediately.

*Yield: 24 hors d'oeuvres*

| | |
|---|---|
| 6 round, thin slices provolone cheese (to be used as a taco shell) | 2 large sliced green peppers |
| | 2 cups alfalfa sprouts |
| | ¼ cup Spicy Yogurt |
| 1 large sliced cucumber | Dressing (see Index) |

## Provolone Tacos

Tuck 2 slices cucumber, 2 slices pepper, and a handful of sprouts into each cheese pocket. Add 1 tablespoon dressing to each taco.

**Yield: 6 servings**

---

| | |
|---|---|
| 24 chunks Havarti cheese or any firm cheese | 1 head chopped romaine lettuce |
| 12 trimmed radishes | |
| 12 chunks green peppers | 1 head chopped iceberg lettuce |
| 12 mushroom caps | |
| 12 pitted black olives | 1 cup shredded carrots |
| 12 ½-inch slices zucchini | 1 cup shredded red cabbage |
| 12 cherry tomatoes | |
| ½ large head cabbage | salad dressing |

## Skewered Salads

Beginning and ending with cheese, thread 12 8-inch skewers with 1 each of radishes, peppers, mushrooms, olives, zucchini, and tomatoes.

Place cabbage head, cutside down, in a large salad bowl or on a platter. Combine romaine, iceberg, carrots, and red cabbage and use this mixture to surround and cover cabbage head. Firmly stick threaded skewers into cabbage head.

To serve, have each person take some mixed salad, 2 skewers, and salad dressing of your choice.

**Yield: 6 servings**

2 cups wheat sprouts
2 cups rye sprouts
2 teaspoons crushed
   caraway seeds

1 small chopped onion
1 tablespoon kelp powder

## Solar Chapatis

### (Wheat and Rye Crackers)

Mix ingredients and put through a food grinder. (It should be sticky but firm.) Roll into 2-inch balls; then press flat. (Place them between 2 plastic bags and roll out with a rolling pin about ⅛ inch thick.)

Place crackers on a mesh or screen in the sunshine, or in a food dryer. The thinner they are rolled, the quicker they dry, and the crisper they are.

*Yield: 12   4-inch crackers*

1 pound ricotta cheese
½ pound farmers cheese
1 tablespoon lemon or lime
   juice
2 egg yolks
1½ pounds finely chopped
   or shredded spinach*

1 cup pine nuts (pignoli)
⅓ cup minced chives
½ cup freshly grated
   Parmesan cheese
3 peeled, sectioned navel
   oranges

## Spinach and Ricotta Balls

In a mixing bowl, beat ricotta cheese, farmers cheese, juice, and egg yolks until thoroughly mixed. Blend in spinach, pine nuts, and chives.

Shape into 6 balls. Sprinkle with Parmesan cheese and surround with orange sections.

*Yield: 6 servings*

*Remove tough stems from spinach before chopping.*

2 cups alfalfa sprouts
½ cup soybean sprouts
½ cup lentil sprouts
½ cup wheat sprouts
¼ cup minced onions
1 minced garlic clove
1 juiced lemon

½ teaspoon kelp powder
1 teaspoon tamari soy sauce
1 sliced avocado
1 sliced tomato
large leaves leaf lettuce or
tender Swiss chard leaves

## Sprout Rolls

Mix sprouts, onions, and garlic. Add lemon juice, kelp, and soy sauce. Place sprout mixture in center of lettuce or Swiss chard leaf and top with avocado and tomato slices. Roll up and secure with a toothpick if necessary.

**Yield: 6-8 servings**

## Vegetable Kebabs

Eye appeal and novelty invite children to snack on these tasty treats. Use vegetables in season and add a slice of cheese for zest.

Start a kebab by spearing a chunk of raw vegetable with 2 toothpicks pushed through its center in opposite directions. Add more chunks to fill up each toothpick, ending perhaps with a raw pea.

Arrange kebabs attractively on a platter and watch them disappear.

# Soups

# Soups

1½ cups almonds    3 cups cold carrot juice
1 garlic clove    1 cup plain yogurt
2 tablespoons olive oil    3 thinly sliced green onions
2 tablespoons lemon juice    1 seeded, chopped green
3 egg yolks      pepper

# Almond and Carrot Gazpacho

Soak almonds in water to cover overnight. Drain. After soaking, the skins may be slipped off if desired.

In an electric blender, process ½ the almonds with garlic, oil, and lemon juice until coarsely chopped. Add egg yolks, remaining almonds, and 1 cup carrot juice, processing until mixture is as smooth as possible.

Unless your blender holds more than 5 cups, it will not be necessary to divide mixture. Pour ½ the mixture into a large measuring cup and set it aside.

Puree remaining ½ with 1 cup carrot juice and pour it into a large jar or container for storage.

Puree remaining mixture that was set aside with remaining cup of carrot juice. Add it to mixture in the storage jar. Cover and chill in the refrigerator.

Before serving, top each portion with a dollop of yogurt. Garnish with onions and peppers.

**Yield: 6 servings**

*Note: If a thinner soup is desired, mixture may be diluted with additional carrot juice or water.*

---

2 cups pitted sweet cherries    ¼ cup honey
2½ cups water    2 tablespoons lemon juice

# Cherry Soup

Process ingredients in an electric blender and liquefy.
Serve chilled.

**Yield: 6 servings**

4½ cups diced zucchini
1½ cups diced cucumbers
¼ cup honey mixed with
    ½ cup water

1½ diced celery stalks
1½ diced green peppers

## Cold Zuke Soup

Process zucchini and cucumbers in an electric blender with ½ the honey-water mixture and blend to a fine puree. Transfer to a bowl.

Process celery, peppers, and the rest of the honey-water mixture in the blender and liquefy. Add cucumber-zucchini mixture and continue processing until a uniform mixture is obtained.

Pour into a bowl and chill in the refrigerator at least 2 hours before serving.

*Yield: 6 servings*

---

1½ cups milk
2 avocadoes
1 medium diced green
    pepper
1 diced onion

1 small grated zucchini
2 tablespoons lemon juice
plain yogurt to taste
Mexican Salsa to taste (see
    Index)

## Cool Green Soup

Process all ingredients but yogurt and salsa in an electric blender until smooth. Add enough yogurt to reach desired consistency.

Serve with a spoonful of salsa as a garnish.

*Yield: 4 cups*

1½ cups soaked, peeled    6 cups carrot juice
         almonds

## Cream of Carrot Soup

Grind almonds into a butter or place them in an electric blender with a small amount of carrot juice and process until very smooth. Add remaining juice and blend into a creamy soup.

**Yield: 6 servings**

---

3 medium peeled, mashed    1¼ cups hot (140°F.)
         tomatoes            water
1 cup corn kernels    ¼ cup sprouts
⅓ cup finely chopped    1 finely chopped green
         celery            onion

## Crunchy Tomato Soup

Mix tomatoes with corn and celery. Pour water over all. Top with sprouts and onions.

**Yield: 6 servings**

---

2 medium peeled, sliced    1 juiced lemon
         cucumbers      mint, parsley, or dill to
4 chopped green onions      taste
1½ cups plain yogurt

## Cucumber-Yogurt Soup

Process ingredients in an electric blender. Blend until smooth. Chill thoroughly before serving.

**Yield: 6 servings**

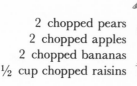

2 chopped pears
2 chopped apples
2 chopped bananas
½ cup chopped raisins

4 juiced oranges
½ cup walnuts or
sunflower seeds

## Fruit Soup

Process fruits in an electric blender with juice and nuts or seeds. Liquefy.

Chill thoroughly before serving.

**Yield: 6 servings**

---

1-2 garlic cloves
1 medium sliced onion
1 sliced cucumber
3 peeled tomatoes
1 seeded green pepper
4 eggs
cayenne pepper to taste

¼ cup vinegar
¼ cup olive oil
¾ cup tomato juice
1 diced cucumber
1 bunch diced green onions
1 chopped green pepper

## Gazpacho

Process the first 5 vegetables and eggs in an electric blender or put vegetables through a food grinder and mix with beaten eggs. Add cayenne pepper and liquids and chill.

To garnish, add diced vegetables to soup just before serving.

**Yield: 6 servings**

2 cups thinly sliced potatoes
1½ cups hot (140°F.) water
1½ cups chopped comfrey
and parsley, your
proportion
1 leaf sweet basil
½ cup chopped green onions

2 sliced okra pods
1 minced garlic clove
1 teaspoon kelp powder
1 tablespoon tamari soy sauce
⅛ teaspoon cayenne
pepper (optional)
sprouts for garnish

## Hearty Potato Soup

Cover potatoes with hot water and set aside.

Remove center rib from comfrey leaves and chop with parsley and basil. Onions and okra may be chopped along with them.

Place all ingredients but potatoes in an electric blender. Pour potato water over them and puree. Add potatoes, using more hot water if necessary, and process until smooth.

Garnish with sprouts and eat with carrot or celery sticks.

**Yield: 4⅔ cups**

---

1 cup peanuts
1 tablespoon olive oil
2 tablespoons lemon juice
2 cups apple juice

2 quartered bananas
3 egg yolks
1 cup raisins
sesame seeds (optional)

## Peanut and Banana Soup

Soak peanuts in water to cover overnight.

In an electric blender, process drained peanuts with oil and lemon juice until coarsely chopped. Gradually add apple juice, processing until mixture is as smooth as possible.

Blend bananas into mixture 1 piece at a time. Blend in egg yolks. Cover mixture and chill thoroughly before serving.

Ladle into soup bowls or crocks and garnish with raisins, and sesame seeds if desired.

**Yield: 6 servings**

*Note: If a thinner soup is desired, mixture may be diluted with additional juice or water.*

1 cup chopped asparagus      ½ cup water
   or broccoli      1 chopped avocado
1 cup chopped mushrooms      ¼ teaspoon tamari soy
1-2 chopped green onions       sauce
  with tops

## Raw Creamed Soup

Process asparagus, mushrooms, and onions in an electric blender, add water according to consistency desired, and liquefy. Stop blender. Add avocado and soy sauce and process.
  Serve at once.

*Yield: 3 cups*

---

6 chopped crookneck      1 cup water
    squash      ½ teaspoon tarragon
1 small sliced onion      ½ teaspoon basil
1 diced celery stalk      1 garlic clove

## Squash Gazpacho

Process ingredients in an electric blender and liquefy.
  Add more water if necessary to achieve desired consistency.

*Yield: 4-6 servings*

---

2 dulse leaves      ground ginger to taste
1 laver or nori      2 tablespoons slivered
3 cups water       almonds
1 cup mung sprouts      2 tablespoons finely sliced
1 cup chopped spinach       mushrooms

## Summer Seas Soup

Soak seaweed in water. Add sprouts and spinach. Season with ginger. Chill.
  Place in 6 individual bowls to serve. Top with almonds and mushrooms.

*Yield: 6 servings*

4 cups strawberries,
  blueberries, or
  raspberries
1 cup plain yogurt
¼ cup honey or to taste

4 cups cold water
1 cup grape juice
½ cup shredded coconut
cashews for garnish

## Summer Soup

Process berries in an electric blender until liquefied. Gently mix in all remaining ingredients but cashews. Chill.

Serve with nuts floating on top.

*Yield: 6 servings*

---

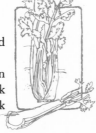

3 medium chopped
  tomatoes
1 chopped red onion
1 chopped leek
1 chopped celery stalk

2 small chopped squash
5 chopped spinach leaves
2 cups water
basil to taste
dill to taste

## Sun-Kissed Vegetable Soup

Combine vegetables in a bowl. Mix in water, basil, and dill.

Prepare in the morning and leave in the sun 4-6 hours before serving.

*Yield: 6 servings*

5 cups plain yogurt
¾ cup half-and-half
2 teaspoons curry powder
(optional)
½ cup water
1 chopped cucumber

1 chopped zucchini
3 thinly sliced green onions
2 chopped tomatoes
½ cup raisins
1 potato
¼ cup chopped dill

## Yogurt-Vegetable Soup

With a whisk, combine yogurt and half-and-half until thoroughly mixed. Dissolve curry powder in a small amount of water; then whisk this mixture and the remaining water into the yogurt mixture.

Add cucumbers, zucchini, onions, tomatoes, and raisins. Mix well, cover, and refrigerate several hours.

Just before serving, peel and grate the potato directly into the yogurt mixture. Ladle soup into 6 bowls and sprinkle with dill.

***Yield: 6 servings***

# Salads

# Salads

# I. Fruit Salads

2 diced apples          ⅓ cup chopped celery
¼ cup chopped raisins   ½ cup mayonnaise
¼ cup chopped nuts      3 halved, peeled avocadoes

## Applacado Salad

Toss lightly all ingredients but avocadoes.
Fill avocadoes with mixture.

*Yield: 6 servings*

---

4 peeled, sliced oranges   ¼ cup chopped pecans or
1 diced apple                  walnuts
1 cup sour cream           pinch nutmeg

## Apple and Orange Salad

Toss ingredients. Chill.

*Yield: 6-8 servings*

---

½ cup raisins            ½ cup chopped peanuts
4 cups chopped cabbage   1 cup shredded cheddar
1 large diced red apple      cheese
2 stalks chopped celery  Sour Cream Dressing

## Cabbage Waldorf Salad
## with Sour Cream Dressing

Soak raisins in hot water to cover for several minutes, rinse in cold water, drain. Combine with cabbage, apples, celery, peanuts, and cheese. Toss with Sour Cream Dressing.

*Yield: 6 servings*

1⅓ cups sour cream   1 teaspoon honey
2 teaspoons vinegar

## Sour Cream Dressing

Mix cream into blended vinegar and honey.

*Yield: 1⅓ cups*

---

3 cups chopped apples   1 cup ½-inch cubes sharp
½ cup chopped nuts         cheese
¼ cup seeds (such as    1 cup mayonnaise or
sunflower or pumpkin)      enough to moisten
½ cup raisins   ½ teaspoon mild curry
1 cup diagonally sliced      powder or to taste
celery   salad greens
1 cup grated carrots

## Curried Waldorf Salad

Toss ingredients with mayonnaise. Season with curry powder to taste. Take it easy with the curry powder; if it needs more, add it ¼ teaspoon at a time.

Serve on salad greens.

*Yield: 6 servings*

---

½ avocado for each serving   lettuce
chilled fruit (melon balls,   lemon-honey dressing
grapes, pineapple, or
berries)

## Fruit on the Half Shell

Fill avocado centers with fruit. Bed halves on lettuce.
Top with dressing of lemon juice and honey mixed in equal parts.

1¼ cups orange juice
9 medium cubed carrots
2¼ cups chopped cabbage
¾ cup raisins

4½ tablespoons sesame
seeds
3 sectioned oranges

## Israeli Carrot Salad

Pour orange juice into an electric blender. Gradually add carrots and puree them.

Transfer mixture to a bowl. Add cabbage, raisins, and seeds. Toss. Garnish with orange sections.

**Yield: 6 servings**

---

3 quartered avocadoes
2 large sectioned grapefruit
2 large sectioned oranges

lettuce leaves
Sour Cream-Date Dressing

## Palm Springs Salad with Sour Cream-Date Dressing

Arrange fruits on lettuce-covered, chilled serving plates. Serve dressing separately.

**Yield: 6-8 servings**

---

1 cup sour cream
½ cup finely chopped dates
½ teaspoon grated orange peel

2 tablespoons orange juice
pinch nutmeg

## Sour Cream-Date Dressing

Combine ingredients. Place in a covered container and chill.

**Yield: 1¾ cups**

1 recipe Peanut and
Banana Soup (see Index)

2 envelopes (2 tablespoons)
unflavored gelatin
½ cup cold water

## Peanut and Banana Gelatin

Make 1 recipe Peanut and Banana Soup but omit raisins.

Sprinkle gelatin over the water in a small heat-resistant cup and let stand 5 minutes to soften. Place cup in a pan of hot (140°F.) water, stirring until gelatin is dissolved. Beat dissolved gelatin into peanut-banana mixture.

Lightly oil a 5- or 6-cup mold and turn mixture into it. Chill until set, about 6 hours. Unmold before serving.

**Yield: 6 servings**

---

6 halved, cored pears
lemon juice to prevent
discoloration
1 cup chopped celery
½ cup chopped walnuts

1 cup raisins
½ cup mayonnaise
1½ cups cottage cheese
salad greens

## Pear Crunch Salad

Sprinkle lemon juice over pears.

Combine celery, walnuts, raisins, mayonnaise, and cottage cheese. Fill pears with mixture.

Serve on salad greens.

**Yield: 6 servings**

3 large halved, peeled,
cored pears
lemon juice to prevent
discoloration
¼ pound Roquefort cheese

¼ cup butter
½ cup plain yogurt
paprika
lettuce leaves

## Pear and Roquefort Salad

Sprinkle lemon juice over pears.

Beat cheese with butter until smooth. Press mixture into pears. Stir yogurt, coat each pear with the dressing, sprinkle with paprika, and chill.

Serve on lettuce leaves.

**Yield: 6 servings**

6 medium apples
3 tablespoons lemon juice
⅜ cup crumbled Roquefort
cheese

4½ tablespoons oil
⅜ cup chopped walnuts
3 tablespoons raisins

## Roquefort Apples

Cut a slice from the top of each apple; reserve. Remove cores and scoop out pulp, leaving ¼-inch shells. Brush shells with juice and dice pulp.

Combine apples and remaining ingredients; toss lightly. Fill shells with mixture and replace tops.

**Yield: 4-6 servings**

1 envelope (1 tablespoon) plus 1 teaspoon unflavored gelatin
¼ cup cold water
1½ cups orange juice, 6 shells reserved
2 tablespoons lemon juice

2 separated eggs
1 cup finely grated carrots
¼ cup chopped golden raisins
½ cup chopped cashews
½ cup alfalfa sprouts or wheat germ for garnish

## Sunshine Souffle

Sprinkle gelatin over the water in a small heat-resistant cup. Let stand 5 minutes to soften. Place in a pan of hot (140°F.) water, stirring until dissolved.

Combine with orange juice, lemon juice, and egg yolks, beating with a rotary mixer until thoroughly mixed.

Chill in the refrigerator, stirring occasionally until mixture mounds when dropped from a spoon. This will take 5–10 minutes to thicken.

Scoop out membrane of 6 largest orange shells with a spoon. Tape a 2-inch, wax-paper collar around each skin.

When juice mixture has reached the consistency of unbeaten egg white, fold in carrots, raisins, and cashews.

Beat egg whites until stiff, but not dry. Fold egg whites into gelatin mixture. Spoon mixture into shells. Chill in the refrigerator until firm.

Remove paper collar before serving. Sprinkle each souffle with alfalfa sprouts or wheat germ.

**Yield: 6 servings**

*Variation: Instead of spooning mixture into orange shells, put it in a 8½ × 4½ × 2½-inch pan to firm. At serving time, cut into squares.*

2 cups grated carrots
½ cup raisins
2 cups diced pineapple
½ cup mayonnaise

1 tablespoon minced onions
1 teaspoon dry mustard
½ teaspoon celery seed
4 lettuce leaves

## Sunshine Special

Combine all ingredients but lettuce. Mix well. Serve on lettuce leaves.

**Yield: 4 servings**

# II. Slaws

| | |
|---|---|
| 6 cups shredded cabbage | Ricotta Dressing |
| 1 cup grated carrots | 2 tablespoons caraway |
| 1 cup chopped celery | seeds (optional) |

## Caraway Coleslaw with Ricotta Dressing

Combine vegetables in a large bowl. Toss with dressing and sprinkle with caraway seeds if desired.

*Yield: 6 servings*

---

| | |
|---|---|
| 8 ounces ricotta cheese | 2 tablespoons oil |
| ¼ cup diced onions | ½ cup plain yogurt |
| 3 tablespoons lemon juice | |

## Ricotta Dressing

In an electric blender, puree the cheese, onions, juice, and oil until creamy.

Add yogurt and blend just until mixed.

*Yield: 2 cups*

---

| | |
|---|---|
| 3 cups shredded green cabbage | 2 medium grated carrots |
| ¾ cup shredded red cabbage | ½ small grated onion |
| 1 cup diagonally slivered green beans | 1 cup coarsely chopped peanuts |
| | Goober Dressing (see recipe below) |

## Goober Slaw

Toss ingredients. Add dressing. Toss again.

*Yield: 6 servings*

| | |
|---|---|
| 1 egg | ½ cup lemon or orange |
| 1 teaspoon honey | juice or cider vinegar |
| ½ teaspoon ground | ½ cup peanut oil |
| mustard seed | 1 tablespoon chopped hot |
| | peppers |

## Goober Dressing

Process ingredients in an electric blender until smooth.

**Yield: 1¾ cups**

---

| | |
|---|---|
| 3 cups grated cabbage | ½ teaspoon celery seed |
| ½ cup grated carrots | ¼ cup cider vinegar |
| 1 cup grated red sweet | 2 tablespoons honey |
| peppers | ⅓ cup mayonnaise |

## Red Cabbage Slaw

In a large bowl, combine cabbage, carrots, peppers, and celery seed.
In a jar, mix remaining 3 ingredients.
Before serving, toss dressing in the salad.

**Yield: 6 servings**

---

| | |
|---|---|
| ½ cup shredded red | 1 small grated parsnip |
| and/or green cabbage | ¼ cup sunflower sprouts |
| 1 medium grated carrot | ½ cup alfalfa sprouts |
| 1 thinly sliced celery stalk | ½ cup bean sprouts (aduki, |
| ½ medium chopped green | mung, and lentil are a |
| pepper | colorful combination) |
| 2 chopped green onions | |

## Sprout Slaw

Toss ingredients with your favorite dressing until well coated. We suggest Cashew Cheese Dressing (see Index). *163*

**Yield: 6 servings**

⅔ cup sour cream
2 tablespoons vinegar
1 tablespoon honey

6 cups pared, grated
   turnips
parsley for garnish

## Turnip Slaw

Combine sour cream, vinegar, and honey. Add dressing to turnips. Garnish with parsley.

*Yield: 6 servings*

---

1 cup shredded cabbage
1 cup shredded carrots
1 cup shredded rutabagas
½ cup grated parsnips
½ cup grated kohlrabi or turnips

1 small thinly sliced red onion
1 cup cottage cheese
½ cup plain yogurt
2 tablespoons wine vinegar
   (optional)

## Winter Slaw

Combine vegetables in a large bowl. In another bowl, stir cottage cheese and yogurt until combined.

Toss salad ingredients and cheese mixture together. Add wine vinegar if desired. Serve immediately.

*Yield: 6 servings*

---

# III. Vegetable Salads

2 heads Boston lettuce
¼ cup thinly sliced water
   chestnuts
4 tablespoons sesame seeds
¼ cup grated Parmesan
   cheese

⅔ cup oil
⅓ cup vinegar
1½ teaspoons tarragon
1 teaspoon honey
½ teaspoon dry mustard
½ crushed garlic clove

## Lettuce with Sesame Seeds

Break lettuce into a bowl and add chestnuts, seeds, and cheese. Toss lightly.

[continued on next page]

To make the dressing, combine remaining ingredients in a small bowl. Mix well and pour as much as needed over salad; toss and taste. Serve at once.

*Yield: 6 servings*

3 cups spinach
1½ cups finely chopped mushrooms
2 chopped green onions

¼ cup Zesty Italian Herb Dressing (see Index)
4 teaspoons sunflower seeds

## Raw Spinach with Mushrooms

Remove stems and center vein from spinach leaves. Tear leaves into bite-size pieces.

Mix spinach, mushrooms, and onions.

Pour dressing over mixture. Marinate 15 minutes.

Just before serving, sprinkle sunflower seeds on each portion.

*Yield: 6 servings*

2 garlic cloves
¾ cup oil
3 tablespoons lemon juice
3 egg yolks
freshly ground black pepper
2 heads bite-size romaine lettuce

2 finely slivered fennel bulbs
1½ cups diced tofu, or ¾ cup tofu and ¾ cup ricotta cheese
1½ cups chopped black walnuts
freshly grated Parmesan cheese

## Romaine and Fennel Salad

Rub garlic in the bottom of a very large wooden salad bowl. Add oil, juice, egg yolks, and pepper. Whisk until well blended.

Add romaine, fennel, tofu, and walnuts; toss lightly until coated with dressing. Sprinkle with cheese.

*Yield: 6 servings*

1 large firm head lettuce
1 tablespoon Roquefort
 cheese
3 tablespoons ground
 carrots
1 tablespoon chopped
 pimentos

2 tablespoons chopped
 green peppers
1½ tablespoons grated
 onions
1 teaspoon lemon juice
¼ cup tomato puree

## Stuffed Lettuce, Country Style

Remove center of lettuce head leaving a good solid shell.

Chop the lettuce heart very fine and mix with remaining ingredients. Pack mixture firmly into lettuce shell. Wrap stuffed lettuce head in wax paper or cheesecloth and chill thoroughly.

Slice into wedges and serve with your favorite dressing.

**Yield: 6 servings**

---

6 cups watercress
¾ cup chopped walnuts
3 tablespoons minced
 onions
3 tablespoons oil

3 teaspoons wine vinegar
¾ teaspoon Herbal
 Mustard (see Index)
freshly ground pepper to
 taste

## Watercress Salad

Remove heavy stems from the watercress. Combine watercress, walnuts, and onions in a bowl.

In a jar, mix oil, vinegar, mustard, and pepper.

Before serving, toss salad with dressing.

**Yield: 6 servings**

# Salad Dressings and Sauces

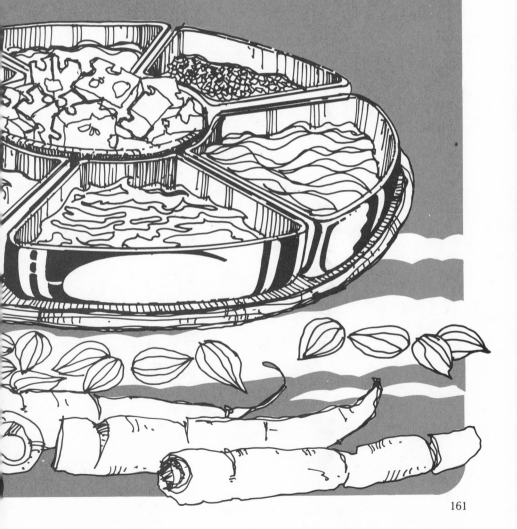

# Salad Dressings and Sauces

# I. Salad Dressings

| | |
|---|---|
| 1 cup sour cream | 2 tablespoons lemon juice |
| ½ cup loosely packed, | 2 tablespoons wine vinegar |
| crumbled blue cheese | black pepper to taste |
| ¼ cup mayonnaise | |

## Blue Cheese Dressing

Process ingredients in an electric blender.
Chill at least 1 hour to blend flavors. Serve over tossed salad greens.

*Yield: 2 cups*

---

| | |
|---|---|
| 1 medium diced carrot | ½ cup oil |
| ½ sliced onion | 4 teaspoons tamari soy |
| 3 tablespoons sesame seeds | sauce |
| 2 tablespoons cider vinegar | ⅞ cup water |

## Carrot Salad Dressing

Process ingredients in an electric blender 5 minutes at high speed.
Use as a salad dressing or pour over vegetables.

*Yield: 2 cups*

---

| | |
|---|---|
| ½ cup Cashew Cheese | 4 radishes |
| Sauce (see Index) | 1 tablespoon poppy seeds |
| ½ cup plain yogurt | 2-3 green onions or chives |
| ¼ cup wine vinegar | |

## Cashew Cheese Dressing

Process ingredients in an electric blender until smooth. Refrigerate
before serving.
Use as a dressing for green salads.

*Yield: 1½ cups*

¼ cup finely slivered   6 tablespoons wine vinegar
        shallots       ¾ cup oil
1 tablespoon Herbal    milk or cream to thin
Mustard (see Index)

## French Housewife's Shallot Dressing

Process ingredients in an electric blender. Cover and keep as long as 2 days. If you put dressing in the refrigerator, use safflower oil, because it stays clear and liquid. Shake to blend again before serving.

Try serving this versatile mayonnaise-shallot sauce as a dip for vegetables. To use the sauce as a salad dressing, thin to the consistency you want with milk or cream.

*Yield: 1 cup*

---

2 mashed bananas    1 teaspoon pure vanilla
2 cups plain yogurt     extract
2 tablespoons honey

## Fruit Salad Dressing

Mix ingredients lightly but thoroughly. Chill.
Serve over any fruit combination.

*Yield: about 2½ cups*

---

2 skinned, quartered   ½ garlic clove
        tomatoes       ½ teaspoon each thyme,
2 tablespoons sunflower    oregano, rosemary, and
        seeds          basil

## Herbed Tomato Dressing

Process ingredients in an electric blender.
Serve on Alfalfa Burgers (see Index).

*Yield: 1 cup*

⅓ cup peanut butter
½ cup peanut oil
1 juiced lemon

1-2 crushed garlic cloves
¼ teaspoon ground red
pepper

## Hot Peanut Butter Dressing

Combine ingredients and mix well.

**Yield: 1 cup**

---

½ cup mayonnaise
½ cup small-curd creamed
cottage cheese
2 tablespoons milk

½ teaspoon grated lime
rind
1 tablespoon lime juice

## Lime Cottage Cheese Dressing

Combine ingredients. Chill.
Serve with orange and grapefruit sections or red onion rings.

**Yield: 1 cup**

---

½ cup creamed cottage
cheese
½ cup buttermilk
½ peeled, seeded lemon

½ chopped green pepper
4 halved radishes
¼ teaspoon paprika
½ minced garlic clove

## Low-Calorie Salad Dressing

Process cottage cheese, buttermilk, and lemon in an electric blender until smooth.

Add remaining ingredients and process until vegetables are finely chopped.

**Yield: 1½ cups**

½ cup peanut butter  ½ cup pineapple juice
½ cup orange juice  3 tablespoons lemon juice

## Peanut Butter-Fruit Dressing

Process ingredients in an electric blender until well blended.
Pour over any fruit salad.

**Yield: 1⅔ cups**

---

⅓ cup peanut butter  ¼ cup honey
¼ cup lime juice  ¼ cup water

## Peanut Dressing

Process ingredients in an electric blender until smooth.

**Yield: 1 cup**

---

⅔ cup chopped pine nuts  pinch nutmeg
(pignoli)  3 tablespoons tarragon
¼ cup olive oil  vinegar
¼ teaspoon grated lemon

## Pine Nut Dressing

Combine ingredients. Mix thoroughly.
Pour over salad greens and toss.

**Yield: 1 cup**

⅔ cup oil  1½ ounces Roquefort cheese
¼ cup wine vinegar  1 tablespoon grated onions
1 medium crumbled bay leaf  black pepper to taste

## Sharp Roquefort Salad Dressing

Combine ingredients in a jar with a tight-fitting lid. Shake until blended. Shake just before serving.
Good with vegetable salads.

**Yield: about 1¼ cups**

---

1 cup sour cream  ¼ teaspoon dry mustard
1½ tablespoons honey  ½ teaspoon celery seeds
1 tablespoon cider vinegar

## Sour Cream Slaw Dressing

Combine ingredients.
Let sit at least 2 hours before mixing with shredded cabbage.

**Yield: 1 cup**

---

1 quart plain yogurt  1 tablespoon minced parsley
1 medium grated onion  1 teaspoon minced dill
3 grated garlic cloves  ½ cup oil
2 teaspoons Barbados  ½ cup tamari soy sauce
molasses or to taste  ½ teaspoon cayenne pepper
2 tablespoons honey or to taste  2 tablespoons apple cider
½ teaspoon celery seed powder  vinegar (optional)
½ teaspoon sage  2 beaten egg yolks (optional)
2 teaspoons thyme

## Spicy Yogurt Dressing

Place yogurt in a large bowl. Grate onion and garlic directly into bowl. With wire whisk gradually blend other ingredients until mixture begins to thicken.
Refrigerate several hours before serving.

**Yield: about 5 cups**

¾ cup sliced strawberries
1 tablespoon honey                    ½ cup mayonnaise

## Strawberry Dressing

Place strawberries in a small bowl. Stir in honey, mashing berries slightly with fork. Add mayonnaise, stirring until well blended.

Chill about 1 hour to develop flavor and color. Serve with fruit salad.

**Yield: 1-1¼ cups**

---

1 egg          2 tablespoons vinegar
½ cup parsley   ¼ cup chopped onions
¼ cup chopped watercress   ¼ cup oil
or spinach     1 tablespoon honey
1 savory sprig

## Summer Salad Dressing

Process ingredients in an electric blender until smooth.

**Yield: 1½ cups**

---

1 cup oil      several chopped or pressed
2 tablespoons tamari soy       garlic cloves
sauce      ½ cup sesame seeds

## Table Mountain Dressing

Mix ingredients thoroughly.
Serve over grated carrots, green salads, or any garden vegetables.

**Yield: about 1¼ cups**

| | |
|---|---|
| 1 cup sesame seeds | 1 peeled, diced lemon |
| ¼ cup water | few drops vinegar |
| 2 minced garlic cloves | 2 tablespoons oil |

## Tahini Salad Dressing

Grind seeds in an electric blender until fine. Add the other ingredients and process until smooth.

**Yield: 1¼ cups**

---

| | |
|---|---|
| ¾ cup cashews | |
| water | 2-3 juiced lemons |
| 2 halved avocadoes | ½ chopped onion |
| 1 medium quartered | ½ teaspoon tamari soy |
| tomato | sauce |

## Vicki's Topper

Place cashews in an electric blender with enough water to cover them. Process until smooth. Add remaining ingredients in the order given and process again.

Serve on salads, sprouts, or as a spread.

**Yield: 1 cup**

---

| | |
|---|---|
| 1 cup plain yogurt | ¼ teaspoon cinnamon |
| 1 teaspoon honey | 2 tablespoons golden raisins |
| ½ teaspoon grated lemon rind | |

## Waldorf Dressing

Mix ingredients. Serve over diced apples and celery.

**Yield: 1 cup**

1 cup plain yogurt
1 cup peeled, seeded, finely
    chopped cucumbers

1 teaspoon finely chopped
    green onions
1 teaspoon minced dill

## Yogurt-Cucumber Dressing

Thoroughly mix ingredients in a small bowl. Cover and chill before serving.

*Yield: 1½ cups*

---

1¼ cups mild-flavored oil
¼ cup crude soy oil (if not
    available, use an equal
    portion of mild oil)
½ cup cider vinegar
10 pressed garlic cloves
1 small finely chopped
    onion
¼ teaspoon celery seed
    powder
¼ teaspoon paprika
2 tablespoons tamari soy
    sauce

1 tablespoon honey
1½ teaspoons molasses
½ teaspoon basil
¼ teaspoon thyme
½ teaspoon oregano
¼-½ cup Parmesan cheese
    (optional)
¼ teaspoon cayenne
    pepper
¼ teaspoon dry mustard

## Zesty Italian Herb Dressing

Combine ingredients in a jar. Shake well.
Refrigerate overnight before serving.

*Yield: 1 pint*

# II. Sauces

6-12 mashed garlic cloves     pepper to taste
4 egg yolks  . 1 cup olive oil
1 tablespoon hot (140°F.)     1¼ cups safflower oil
water     1 tablespoon lemon juice

## *Aioli Sauce*

### (French Garlic Mayonnaise)

Place garlic in a large round-bottom bowl and add egg yolks. Start beating with a wire whisk, or rotary or electric beater. Add water and pepper.

Then add oil drop by drop, beating constantly until more than ½ the oil is used. (If using a manual rotary beater, you may need a second person to drip the oil.) The rest of the oil may be added in larger quantities. The sauce should get thicker as the oil increases. When all oil has been added, beat in lemon juice.

Use as a dip or salad dressing.

*Yield: 2 cups*

---

¼ cup apple cider or your     3 diced apples
favorite fruit juice

## *Applesauce*

Gradually add apples to the juice and process in an electric blender until smooth.

*Yield: 2 cups*

---

## *Bucky's Horseradish*

Pull horseradish roots. Scrub well. Cut roots into small pieces, about ½ inch. Pack pieces into a large plastic bag and freeze, at least overnight.

*[continued on next page]*

When relish is needed, take a small handful of cut roots and chop in blender, without thawing. Add an equal amount of vinegar and a small amount of milk (1 teaspoon per pint).

The relish is then ready for table or jars.

---

½ cup cashew pieces   water

## Cashew Cheese Sauce

Soak cashews in water to cover overnight.

Process cashews and water in an electric blender so that they form a paste.

Place in a small bowl, cover, and let stand 24 hours at room temperature, or warmer. (This produces a slight fermentation.)

*Yield: ½ cup*

---

1 well-beaten egg
1 tablespoon vinegar
1 tablespoon oil
2 teaspoons freshly ground mustard seed
¼ teaspoon tamari soy sauce

¼ teaspoon arrowroot
2 teaspoons finely chopped herbs (such as dill, chervil, green onion, cayenne)

## Herbal Mustard

Combine ingredients in an electric blender and mix well. Pour into a double boiler and heat gently, while stirring, until mixture thickens to desired consistency.

Store in the refrigerator in a sealed container. A lemon slice on top will help maintain freshness.

*Yield: ⅓ cup*

2 room temperature egg    1 cup oil
yolks    1 tablespoon lemon juice
1 teaspoon vinegar    ½ teaspoon dry mustard

## Homemade Mayonnaise

Warm a small bowl. Add egg yolks and vinegar and beat lightly with a whisk or electric beater set at medium speed. Add ¼ cup oil drop by drop, beating constantly. When mixture starts to thicken, add the remaining oil 1 tablespoon at a time, beating well after each addition.

Add juice and mustard. Beat until well combined.

Place in a glass container, cover, and store in the refrigerator.

**Yield: about 1 cup**

Note: Mayonnaise will keep 4-6 weeks if stored properly.

# Main Dishes

# Main Dishes

# I. Cheese and Yogurt

¾ cup olive oil
2 tablespoons lemon juice
1 cup firmly packed basil
leaves
1 minced garlic clove
1 cup sunflower seeds

¼ pound tofu
¾ cup freshly grated
Parmesan cheese
3 large halved avocadoes
tomato slices for garnish

## Avocadoes Stuffed with Basil

Process oil, juice, basil, and garlic in an electric blender until smooth. Add seeds and process again. Next, add tofu and process. Add cheese and process until smooth.

Spoon pureed mixture into avocado halves. Surround with tomato slices.

**Yield: 6 servings**

---

3 medium zucchini
½ pound thinly sliced
Gruyere cheese
½ cup chopped black
walnuts

Curried Yogurt Dressing
(see recipe below)
3 large halved avocadoes
1 cup alfalfa sprouts

## Avocadoes Stuffed with Zucchini, Cheese, and Walnuts

Grate zucchini into a bowl using the coarse side of a grater.

Cut cheese slices into julienne strips about 1½ inches long. Add cheese strips and walnuts to zucchini and toss lightly with just enough dressing to coat.

Fill avocadoes with filling. Sprinkle with sprouts.

**Yield: 6 servings**

1 teaspoon curry powder     1 cup plain yogurt
1 tablespoon lemon juice     1 tablespoon minced dill

## Curried Yogurt Dressing

Mix curry powder with juice and stir into yogurt. Stir in dill.

**Yield: about 1 cup**

*Note: Any leftover dressing will keep in the refrigerator 3-4 days if covered.*

---

⅔ cup minced broccoli     ⅓ cup plain yogurt
    heads     ¼ cup ground filberts
1⅓ cups grated carrots     ¼ cup ground sunflower
1 cup ground blanched         seeds
    almonds

## Brocc-Al-Loaf

Combine broccoli, carrots, and almonds in a bowl. Add yogurt and mix thoroughly. Mold into loaf shape. Chill.
Sprinkle nuts and seeds on slices before serving.

**Yield: 6 servings**

---

6 large round green     ½-¾ cup crumbled blue
    peppers         cheese
1 envelope (1 tablespoon)     ¼ cup chopped chives
    unflavored gelatin     ¼ cup chopped parsley
¼ cup cold water     5 cups shredded carrots
3 cups creamed cottage     1 cup seedless raisins
    cheese

## Cheese and Pepper Wedge Salad

Hollow peppers by using a sharp knife to cut around the stems. Remove seeds without splitting the sides of the peppers. Wash and place upside down to drain.

[continued on next page]

Sprinkle gelatin over the water in a small heat-resistant cup and let stand 5 minutes to soften. Place cup in a pan of hot (140°F.) water, stirring until gelatin is dissolved.

In a large mixing bowl, combine dissolved gelatin with cottage cheese, blue cheese, chives, and parsley and beat with a rotary or electric mixer until ingredients are thoroughly mixed.

Spoon gelatin mixture into pepper shells, place upright in the refrigerator, and chill until set, about 3 hours.

Combine carrots and raisins and divide among 6 serving plates. Cut each filled pepper into 4–6 wedges and arrange on carrot beds in a circular pattern.

*Yield: 6 servings*

| | |
|---|---|
| ½ head shredded red cabbage | 3 seeded, chopped tomatoes |
| 2 thinly sliced green peppers | 3 grated carrots |
| 2 thinly sliced red peppers | 1 cup alfalfa sprouts |
| 5 chopped green onions | 8 ounces grated mozzarella cheese |

## Cheesy Sprout Combo

Place ingredients in a large bowl, top with your favorite dressing, and toss gently.

*Yield: 6 servings*

| | |
|---|---|
| 2 cups cottage cheese | ¼ teaspoon paprika |
| 1 tablespoon finely chopped onions | ¼ cup chopped radishes |
| 1 cup chopped nuts | 1½ teaspoons lemon juice |
| | lettuce leaves |

## Cottage Cheese Loaf

Mix ingredients. Press into a 4×8-inch loaf pan. Chill until firm. Cut into slices and serve on lettuce leaves.

*Yield: 4-6 servings*

| | |
|---|---|
| 3 cups cottage cheese | 2 small thinly sliced zucchini |
| 1 cup chopped black walnuts | 3 thinly sliced (tender part) |
| 2 tablespoons finely | green onions |
| chopped parsley | 6 thinly sliced radishes |
| 2 tablespoons snipped chives | ½ cup Table Mountain |
| 2 teaspoons curry powder | Dressing (see Index) |
| ½ head bite-size romaine lettuce | 6 large tomatoes |
| 2 chopped Belgian endives | ½ cup alfalfa sprouts |

## Curried Cottage Cheese in Tomato Flowers

Combine cottage cheese, walnuts, parsley, chives, and curry, blending thoroughly. Let chill in the refrigerator at least 1 hour to mellow.

In a large mixing bowl, combine romaine, endive, zucchini, onions, and radishes and toss lightly with dressing.

Slice stem ends off the tomatoes and place them outside down on a cutting board. Cut each tomato into 6 wedge slices, but only to within 1 inch of the bottom. (Do not slice through all the way.) Spread out the sections to form each tomato into a flower.

Divide dressed salad among 6 individual bowls and place a tomato flower in the center of each. Spoon a portion of cheese mixture into the center of each tomato and sprinkle sprouts over cheese.

**Yield: 6 servings**

---

| | |
|---|---|
| 2 envelopes (2 tablespoons) | 1 cup plain yogurt |
| unflavored gelatin | 2 tablespoons lemon juice |
| ½ cup cold water | 1 peeled, pressed garlic clove |
| 4 cups (4 medium) mashed | ½ cup chopped cucumbers |
| avocadoes | 1 large chopped tomato |

## Guacamole Mold

Sprinkle gelatin over the water in a small heat-resistant cup and let stand 5 minutes to soften. Place cup in a pan of hot (140°F.) water, stirring until gelatin is dissolved.

[continued on next page]

In a large mixing bowl, add gelatin to avocadoes, yogurt, juice, and garlic. Beat until thoroughly mixed.

Chill until slightly thickened and mixture forms a mound when dropped from a spoon. Fold in cucumbers and tomatoes.

Turn into an oiled 6-cup mold and chill until firm, preferably overnight. Unmold before serving.

*Yield: 6 servings*

---

2 heads romaine lettuce
6 large thickly sliced
  tomatoes
2 large sliced red onions

1 pound sliced mozzarella
  cheese
Herb Sauce
1½ cups pine nuts (pignoli)

## Italian Vegetable Plate with Herb Sauce

Separate romaine into leaves. Place in a large bowl.

Alternate tomato, onion, and mozzarella slices on leaves.

Pour enough sauce to taste and sprinkle each serving with ¼ cup pine nuts.

*Yield: 6 servings*

---

1½ cups olive oil
¾ cup pine nuts (pignoli)
3 large peeled garlic cloves
1½ cups basil leaves
1½ cups parsley, stems
  removed

1 cup spinach, stems
  removed
¾ cup freshly grated
  Parmesan cheese
¼ cup cider vinegar

## Herb Sauce

Process ingredients in an electric blender until smooth.

*Yield: about 5 cups*

½ pound thinly sliced
Swiss cheese
4 celery stalks
6 small thinly sliced button
mushrooms
3 tablespoons chia seeds

¼ cup oil
¼ cup cider vinegar
3 large halved avocadoes
3 tablespoons finely
chopped parsley

## Julienne Stuffed Avocadoes

Cut cheese slices into julienne strips about 1½ inches long.

Remove strings from the celery and cut it into pieces about 1½ inches long; then cut pieces lengthwise into thin julienne strips.

Combine cheese, celery, mushrooms, and seeds in a large mixing bowl. Add oil and vinegar and toss lightly.

Fill avocadoes with vegetables. Garnish with parsley.

*Yield: 6 servings*

---

6 large lettuce leaves
½ cup (4 ounces) dry
cottage cheese or farmers
cheese
2 finely chopped green
peppers

4 finely shredded carrots
¼ cup chopped walnuts
minced onion and garlic to
taste
½ teaspoon crushed basil
6 pimento strips

## Lettuce Leaf Rolls

Spread each lettuce leaf with a layer of cheese. Sprinkle peppers, carrots, walnuts, and seasonings on top.

Roll up the leaves using toothpicks to hold them together. Or when in season, tie the rolls with clover blossoms so that the flowers are on top.

Garnish rolls with pimento.

*Yield: 6 servings*

3 large halved papayas
1 cup soybean grits
1½ cups pineapple juice

1 cup plain yogurt
alfalfa sprouts for garnish
dark green lettuce leaves

## Papayas Stuffed with Grits

Scoop seeds from papayas. Reserve 3 tablespoons seeds and pound them to a powder in a mortar with a pestle. In a mixing bowl, combine powdered seeds with grits; add juice, stirring to mix, and let stand 15-20 minutes.

Fill papayas with grit-juice mixture. Top each with a dollop of yogurt and a generous sprinkle of sprouts.

Serve on lettuce leaves.

***Yield: 6 servings***

---

1½ cups cottage cheese
⅔ cup mayonnaise
2 small crushed garlic cloves
1 pound french-style green
beans

2 cups shredded cheddar
cheese
lettuce leaves

## Quick Summer Beans

Process cottage cheese, mayonnaise, and garlic in an electric blender until smooth.

Mix beans, cheddar cheese, and blended ingredients.

Serve on lettuce leaves.

***Yield: 6 servings***

1 cup cottage cheese
1 teaspoon honey
1 teaspoon crushed or
powdered chia seeds
2 cups shredded cabbage
⅛ cup finely chopped
green onions

1 teaspoon minced parsley
1 tablespoon chopped
chives
1 medium grated red beet
1½ cups chopped lettuce
leaves

## Red Cottage Cheese

Mix cheese, honey, and seeds thoroughly.

In a separate bowl, combine remaining ingredients. Toss with cottage cheese mixture.

**Yield: 3 cups**

---

2 cups chopped walnuts
4 tablespoons softened
butter
½ teaspoon dry mustard
(more if you like things
hot)

1 cup plain yogurt or
cottage cheese, whipped
until creamy
6 ounces finely chopped spinach
3 ounces chopped
mushroom caps

## Spinach Pie

In a 9-inch pie plate, mix nuts and butter, blending well. Press mixture evenly on bottom and sides of pie plate to form crust. Chill at least 1 hour.

Add enough water to mustard to make a paste. In a small bowl, mix yogurt and mustard.

Mix spinach, mushrooms, and sauce and fill chilled piecrust with mixture. Cover and return to refrigerator for another hour before serving.

**Yield: 1   9-inch pie**

*Note: If you dip bottom of pie plate in warm water about 1 minute before serving, pie will be easier to remove from plate.*

½ cup mung sprouts
8 chopped green onions
   with tops
¼ cup lentil sprouts

4 cups cottage cheese
¼ cup sliced mushrooms
lettuce leaves

## Sprouts 'n' Cheese

Mix ingredients.
Serve on lettuce leaves.

**Yield: 4-6 servings**

---

½ cup garbanzo sprouts
1 cup solidly packed alfalfa sprouts
½ cup torn-up spinach
½ cup torn-up lettuce
½ cup sliced green onions
1 cup chopped green peppers
½ cup peas

¾ cup diced squash
½ cup chopped cucumbers
⅔ cup cubed sharp
   cheddar cheese
Tart Salad Dressing (see
   recipe below)

## Sprouts, Vegetables, and Cheese

Combine ingredients in a large bowl. Just before serving, toss with dressing.

**Yield: 6 servings**

---

¼ cup oil      pinch cayenne pepper
¼ cup vinegar  1 minced garlic clove

## Tart Salad Dressing

Combine ingredients in a jar; shake well.

**Yield: ½ cup**

2 heads finely chopped red
   leaf lettuce
3 cups sliced zucchini
3 cups sliced yellow
   summer squash
1 cup baby peas

1 cup sliced button
   mushrooms
Peanut Butter-Tofu
   Dressing
1 grated carrot

## Squash with Peanut Butter-Tofu Dressing

Place lettuce in 6 salad bowls.

In a large bowl, combine zucchini, squash, peas, and mushrooms. Toss with dressing.

Place a portion of coated vegetables on each lettuce bed. Sprinkle with carrots and serve.

***Yield: 6 servings***

---

¼ pound tofu
½ cup peanut butter

½ cup plain yogurt

## Peanut Butter-Tofu Dressing

Process ingredients in an electric blender until fluffy. Serve atop salad.

***Yield: 1¼ cups***

---

½ pound chilled ripe Brie
   or Camembert cheese
3 ounces room temperature
   ricotta cheese
2 tablespoons room
   temperature butter

2 tablespoons snipped
   chives
⅓ cup pine nuts (pignoli)
1 large bunch celery

## Stuffed Celery Wheels

Remove crust from the Brie while it is cold (it will be easier to handle). Place cheese in a large mixing bowl and allow to reach room

[continued on next page]

temperature so that it is of spreading consistency. Add ricotta and butter, and cream mixture until smooth. Stir in chives and pine nuts.

Cut a slice off the top of the celery to remove the leafy ends. Cut a slice off the bottom so that the stalks are loose. Separate stalks and wash them. Remove any strings and dry stalks with paper towels.

Stuff stalks with cheese mixture. Starting with the center stalks, re-shape the celery bunch. Wrap stuffed bunch tightly in aluminum foil and chill.

When firmly set, cut the bunch into ½-inch slices. Allow 2 slices per person.

May be served on a bed of shredded carrots if desired.

*Yield: 6-8 servings*

---

| 6 halved lengthwise, seeded cucumbers | 4 thinly sliced green onions |
| 1½ cups peas | ½ cup finely diced tofu |
| 1 cup chopped black walnuts | 1 cup plain yogurt |
| | ¼ cup snipped dill |
| | 6 cups shredded carrots |

## Stuffed Cucumber Boats

In a mixing bowl, combine peas, walnuts, onions, tofu, yogurt, and dill. Toss lightly to mix.

Fill cucumber halves with stuffing.

Spread 1 cup shredded carrots on each serving plate. Top each carrot bed with 2 stuffed cucumbers.

*Yield: 6 servings*

2 bars (6 ounces each)
chilled Crema Dania
cheese
3 ounces room temperature
cream cheese or ricotta
cheese
3 tablespoons room
temperature butter

½ cup black walnuts,
soaked overnight in
water, dried, and
chopped
¼ cup finely chopped
parsley
¼ cup finely chopped
green onions
6 medium Belgian endives

## Stuffed Endive

Remove crust from the Crema Dania while it is cold. Place cheese in a large mixing bowl until it reaches room temperature. Cream it with cream cheese and butter until mixture is smooth. Stir in walnuts, parsley, and onions.

Slice off ½ inch from the bottom of each endive and pull off 7-8 leaves from each, being careful not to break leaves. Keep each group of separated leaves together with its center heart so that they can easily be matched back into place after stuffing.

Mark cheese mixture into 6 portions. Fill each group of separated leaves with a dab of mixture and spread to coat the inside of leaf evenly. When all leaves have been filled, start with smallest leaves and reassemble each endive. Wrap each tightly in foil and chill at least 4 hours.

To serve, cut 3-4   ¾-inch slices from bottom end of each endive. Arrange slices around remaining point of the endive.

May be served on a bed of shredded or grated vegetables if desired.

**Yield: 6 servings**

6 large green peppers
4½ cups alfalfa sprouts
¾ cup finely diced onions

¾ cup shredded sharp
cheddar cheese
¾ cup mayonnaise or
enough to moisten

## Stuffed Peppers

Cut tops off peppers and clean out membranes and seeds.
Mix remaining ingredients thoroughly.
Stuff peppers with mixture. Chill.

**Yield: 6 servings**

| | |
|---|---|
| 12 medium Italian sweet peppers | ⅔ cup chopped tomatoes |
| | ¼ cup minced chives |
| ½ cup farmers cheese | ½ cup chopped celery |
| ½ cup cottage cheese | ½ cup chopped Brazil nuts |
| 1 egg yolk | 3 cups shredded carrots for garnish |
| 1 cup young corn kernels | |

## Summer Stuffed Peppers

Slice off stem end of peppers and remove insides. Wash and drain upside down.

In a mixing bowl, beat farmers cheese, cottage cheese, and egg yolk until thoroughly mixed.

In a second bowl, combine corn, tomatoes, chives, celery, and nuts. Fold into cheese mixture. Stuff peppers with filling.

Allow 2 stuffed peppers for each serving and garnish with ½ cup shredded carrots.

*Yield: 6 servings*

---

| | |
|---|---|
| 3 cups shredded cabbage | 1 cup crumbled blue cheese |
| 1½ cups alfalfa sprouts | 1 cup plain yogurt |
| 3 cups cored, unpeeled, chopped apples | ¼ cup caraway seeds (optional) |
| 3 tablespoons lemon juice | ½–1 cup chopped walnuts (optional) |
| ½ pound mashed tofu | |

## Tofu Alfalfa Slaw with Apples

In a large mixing bowl, combine cabbage and sprouts. Mix apples with juice and add them to the bowl.

In another bowl, combine tofu, blue cheese, and yogurt, mixing well. Add to vegetables and toss until coated. Sprinkle with caraway seeds and walnuts if desired.

*Yield: 6 servings as a side dish*
*3 servings as an entree*

# II. Fish

1 pound filleted flounder
10 juiced lemons
4 tablespoons oil
4 skinned, diced tomatoes
1 diced cucumber

1 large minced onion
½ teaspoon oregano
black pepper to taste
2 sliced avocadoes

## *Ceviche*

### (Seafood Cocktail)

Cut fish into small squares. Place in a china or glass dish; pour lemon juice over all; cover and refrigerate 12 hours, occasionally turning fish pieces with a wooden spoon. Drain juice from fish.

Add oil, vegetables, and seasonings to fish.

Serve ice cold in sherbet glasses or shells, garnished with a slice of avocado.

*Yield: 6 servings*

---

¾ pound salmon
1 juiced lime
3 medium peeled, finely
chopped tomatoes

¼ cup minced onions
3 peeled, halved lengthwise
cucumbers

## Cucumbers Stuffed with Salmon

Marinate salmon in lime juice. Cover and refrigerate overnight.

Remove skin and bones, and using your fingers, shred fish finely. Squeeze shreds with your fingertips until they are the consistency of pulp. Work tomatoes and onions into mixture. Cover and refrigerate while preparing the cucumbers.

Hollow cucumbers by scooping out seeds with a spoon. Stuff cucumbers with salmon filling. Allow ½ per person.

*Yield: 6 servings*

| 1½ pounds red snapper, | 1 finely chopped green |
| sea bass, or tuna | pepper |
| ½ cup lime juice | 1 chopped tomato |
| ¼ cup minced onions | 1 cup Coconut Milk (see |
| 1 grated carrot | recipe below) |

## Marinated Fish Tahitian Style

Cut fish into 1 × 2-inch slices and place in a mixing bowl. Add lime juice and stir. Cover and marinate in the refrigerator 2–3 hours.

Drain off all but a small amount of marinade. Add vegetables and stir.

Pour Coconut Milk over mixture and serve immediately in individual bowls or crocks.

**Yield: 6 servings**

---

| 1 cup grated coconut | 1 cup very hot water |

## Coconut Milk

Place coconut in a mixing bowl; add water and let stand 30 minutes. Squeezing to extract all liquid, knead thoroughly and strain mixture through cheesecloth.

Place in a glass jar, cover, and chill in the refrigerator a few hours before serving.

**Yield: about 1 cup**

---

| 2-pound slice firm-fleshed | 4 shredded carrots |
| fish (swordfish, tuna, cod, | 1 tablespoon grated ginger |
| halibut, or salmon) | Dipping Sauce |
| 4 shredded turnips | |

## Raw Fish with Dipping Sauce

Clean, scale, and remove bones from fish. Cut fish straight down into ½-inch slices; then cut slices into ½-inch cubes. Divide fish among 6 plates.

Arrange turnips and carrots around fish as a garnish. Sprinkle fish with ginger.

Serve immediately with sauce.

**Yield: 6 servings**

---

¼ cup tamari soy sauce      1 thinly sliced (tender part)
¼ cup lime juice            green onion

## Dipping Sauce

Combine liquids in a small bowl. Float onions on top.

**Yield: ½ cup**

---

1½ pounds center-cut       1 tablespoon crushed
   salmon                     peppercorns
1 cup chopped dill       3 halved lemons and dill
2 tablespoons fennel seeds    sprigs for garnish
2 teaspoons honey     Mustard Sauce (see recipe

## Salmon Marinated with Dill

### (A favorite Swedish recipe)

Cut salmon in half lengthwise and remove bones. Wipe with a damp cloth.

Lay ½ the fish skinside down in a glass or enamel dish (do not use metal) and sprinkle with dill and fennel. Combine honey and pepper-corns in a small bowl and sprinkle mixture over dill. Top with the other ½ fish skinside up. If thickness of fish is uneven, turn the top piece around so that the thick end on top is over the thin end of the bottom and the salmon lies fairly flat.

Cover dish with plastic wrap and place a cutting board on top. Place 3-4 cans of food on cutting board to weigh it down.

*[continued on next page]*

Refrigerate salmon 48–72 hours, turning it over every 12 hours. When turning, baste inside and out with the marinade that accumulates. Replace weights each time.

To serve, remove salmon from marinade and scrape off dill and seasonings with a spoon. Pat dry with paper towels.

Place salmon skinside down on a cutting board. Cut flesh into thin slices and detach each slice from the skin.

Lay slices overlapping on each plate and garnish with lemon and dill.

Serve with sauce.

*Yield: 6 servings*

---

| | |
|---|---|
| ⅔ cup olive oil | 1 teaspoon mustard seed |
| ⅓ cup lemon juice | ¼ teaspoon freshly ground |
| 1 tablespoon honey | pepper |

## Mustard Sauce

Blend ingredients in an electric blender and allow to stand 1 hour in the refrigerator before serving.

*Yield: 1 cup*

---

| | |
|---|---|
| 2 pounds ½-inch cubes flounder, scrod, or sole fillets | 1 minced garlic clove |
| | 2 tablespoons chopped parsley |
| ¼ cup chopped onions | 1 tablespoon chopped basil |
| ⅓ cup lime juice | 1 finely chopped sweet red pepper |
| ½ cup tomato juice | |
| ⅓ cup olive oil | chicory for garnish |

## Spicy Marinated Fish Fillets

Combine all ingredients but chicory in a mixing bowl. Cover and refrigerate 8–12 hours.

Serve on a bed of chicory.

*Yield: 6 servings*

2 cups soaked grain (see
Index)
¼ cup rice vinegar
2 tablespoons tamari soy
sauce
6 laver sheets (dried
seaweed — nori in
Japanese, kyi choy in
Chinese)

½ pound thinly sliced tuna
freshly grated ginger
finely shredded carrots and
lettuce for garnish

## Sushi with Grain

Combine vinegar and soy sauce and mix with soaked grain. On a bamboo rolling mat or cloth napkin, place a sheet of laver. Spread it evenly with a portion of vinegared grain, but leaving a 2-inch margin at one end. About 1 inch down from the edge of laver, arrange a row of fish. Sprinkle with a small amount of ginger.

With the help of the bamboo mat, and starting at the grain end, roll sushi into a compact roll. Follow the same procedure with each laver sheet.

Cut each filled roll into 1½-inch slices. Garnish with vegetables.

**Yield: 6 servings**

---

1½ pounds cubed swordfish
½ cup lime juice
12 pearl onions
12 cherry tomatoes

12 button mushrooms
salad greens for garnish
Dill Dressing (see recipe
below)

## Swordfish Shish

Marinate fish in juice. Cover and refrigerate 6–8 hours. Drain and discard liquid.

On 12 skewers, alternate cubes of marinated swordfish, onions, tomatoes, and mushrooms.

Place on a bed of salad greens. Serve with dressing.

**Yield: 6 servings**

¾ cup olive oil   1 tablespoon snipped dill
¼ cup lemon juice   1 halved garlic clove
½ teaspoon dry mustard

## Dill Dressing

The day before serving, combine ingredients in a jar. Cover and refrigerate overnight.
Discard garlic before serving.

**Yield: 1 cup**

---

1½ pounds skinless,   1 tablespoon crushed
boneless fish fillets (such   peppercorns
as tuna, striped bass, or   lime slices for garnish
weakfish)   parsley sprigs for garnish
2 tablespoons lime juice

## Thon au Poivre Vert

**(Raw tuna with peppercorns)**

Place fillets on a flat surface and slice diagonally into very thin slices. Arrange slices in 1 layer and slightly overlapping on a chilled platter. Sprinkle with lime juice. Smear peppercorns over fish. Garnish with lime and parsley.

**Yield: 6 servings**

---

# III. Fruits and Vegetables

4 avocadoes   1 cup grated carrots
2 juiced lemons   1 cup finely chopped cabbage
1 teaspoon basil   4 tablespoons diced onions
½ teaspoon sage   4 tablespoons chopped parsley
dash cayenne pepper   sprouts or salad greens
4 cups finely chopped celery   1¼ cups ground almonds

## Avocado-Almond Loaf

Mash avocadoes with lemon juice, then blend in seasonings. Mix vegetables with avocado mixture.

Place on a bed of sprouts or greens. Top with ground almonds.

*Yield: 6–8 servings*

2½ cups mung sprouts
3½ cups chopped broccoli
   stems and florets
1 cup sliced celery

¼ cup sesame oil
2 tablespoons tamari soy
   sauce
1 teaspoon honey

## Broccoli and Sprouts

Combine sprouts and vegetables.
Mix oil, soy sauce, and honey. Toss with vegetables.

*Yield: 6 servings*

5 cups fruit (such as apples,
   pears, or berries)
4 tablespoons lemon juice
1 teaspoon honey,
depending on sweetness
   of fruit

1 cup oat sprouts
1 cup sunflower seeds
½ cup wheat germ

## Fresh Fruit and Sprouts

Combine fruit and juice, adding honey to sweeten as desired.
Mix with sprouts, seeds, and wheat germ.

*Yield: 6 servings*

2 bunches trimmed
radishes
6 small ½-inch slices
zucchini
3 dozen button mushrooms
1 pound ½ × 3-inch slices
cheddar cheese

Avocado Sauce
3 tablespoons minced
parsley
3 tablespoons chopped
sweet red peppers

## Jardiniere Platter with Avocado Sauce

Place a small custard cup in the center of each serving plate. Divide and arrange radishes, zucchini, mushrooms, and cheddar fingers in piles around cups.

Spoon a portion of sauce into each cup and garnish sauce with parsley and peppers.

*Yield: 6 servings*

2 large avocadoes
3 tablespoons lemon or
lime juice

¼ cup mayonnaise
1 tablespoon finely minced onion
2 tablespoons oil

## Avocado Sauce

Mash avocadoes with a fork. Add remaining ingredients and mix thoroughly.

Serve immediately.

*Yield: about 1¾ cups sauce*

3 cups diced avocadoes
3 cups diced tomatoes
3 chopped green onions
2 tablespoons oil
2 tablespoons cider vinegar

1 tablespoon chopped
oregano leaves
2 tablespoons sunflower
seeds
2 tablespoons sesame seeds

## Mardi Gras Refresher

Place avocadoes in a large mixing bowl.

Add remaining ingredients. Toss gently.

*Yield: 6 servings*

| | |
|---|---|
| ¼ cup tamari soy sauce | 1 head cauliflower florets |
| 1 cup water | 2 medium chunked broccoli |
| ½ cup red wine vinegar | stalks |
| 4 garlic cloves | ½ pound halved |
| 4 ginger slices (optional) | mushrooms |
| 2 medium chunked | 1 cake tofu |
| zucchini | |

## Marinated Vegetables

Mix soy sauce, water, vinegar, garlic, and ginger in a medium-size bowl.

Place vegetables and tofu in a large bowl. Pour sauce over the vegetables.

Allow vegetables to sit no longer than 2 hours. Toss them occasionally.

Drain before serving.

*Yield: 6 servings*

---

| | |
|---|---|
| 1 sweet potato | 1 pound peanuts |
| 1 onion | 2 tablespoons horseradish |
| 1 carrot | or to taste |
| 1 white potato | parsley and sprouts for |
| 1 turnip | garnish |
| 1 beet | |
| 3-4 stalks celery with | |
| leaves | |

## Raw Vegetable Loaf

Put each vegetable and the peanuts through a food grinder, then mix all together thoroughly.

Season by mixing in horseradish. Press into a loaf pan and refrigerate.

Turn out onto a platter and garnish with parsley and sprouts.

*Yield: 4-6 servings*

| | |
|---|---|
| 1 medium solid head cabbage | 3 tablespoons mayonnaise |
| 12 soaked, drained dried figs | 1 teaspoon freshly ground pepper |
| 2 carrots | ½ teaspoon dry mustard |
| 2 tablespoons grated onions | 3 tablespoons vinegar |
| 2 parsley sprigs | ½ cup whipped heavy cream |
| 1 teaspoon celery seed | soaked figs and small lettuce leaves for garnish |
| 1 cup chopped pineapple | |

## San Jose Highlights

Cut the stem at the bottom of cabbage to make an even base. Cut out the center. Scoop out all possible cabbage, but retain a good shell that will not leak.

Remove stems from the figs.

Put the scooped-out cabbage, figs, carrots, onions, and parsley through a food grinder using the coarse screen.

Place mixture in a large bowl. Add celery seed, pineapple, mayonnaise, pepper, mustard, and vinegar and stir lightly. Fold whipped cream into salad.

Spoon into the cabbage shell, heaping high. Garnish with more figs and lettuce.

*Yield: 6 servings*

| | |
|---|---|
| 2 cups grated carrots | ½ cup blanched, chopped almonds |
| ½ cup sunflower meal | ½ cup sesame seeds |
| ½ cup cashew meal | 1 cup chopped red pepper |
| ½ cup finely chopped peanuts | 1 cup minced parsley |
| ½ cup finely chopped pumpkin seeds | 2 tablespoons crushed basil |
| 1 cup finely chopped tomatoes | 3 tablespoons caraway seeds |
| 1 small finely grated beet | 1 tablespoon tamari soy sauce |

## Vegetable Marvel Loaf

Mix ingredients thoroughly and form into loaf.
Chill and slice.

*Yield: 6 servings*

1 cup sesame seeds
1 cup sunflower seeds
½ cup almonds
½ cup walnuts
½ cup chopped green pepper
1 cup corn kernels
4 chopped medium tomatoes
½ cup chopped green onions
2 tablespoons tamari soy sauce
1 minced garlic clove
lettuce, parsley, watercress, or sprouts
Cucumber Dip (see Index)

## Vegetarian Liver Pate

Separately grind seeds, almonds, and walnuts in a food grinder or blender. Mix them together in a medium-size bowl. Add peppers, corn, tomatoes, onions, soy sauce, and garlic and mix thoroughly.

Press mixture firmly into an oiled 3-4 cup ring mold. Chill until firm.

Unmold onto a bed of lettuce, parsley, watercress, or sprouts. Serve with sauce.

**Yield: 4⅔ cups**

---

# IV. Gelatin

2 envelopes (2 tablespoons) unflavored gelatin
½ cup cold water
⅓ cup lemon or lime juice
2 cups beet juice
1 cup plain yogurt
2 cups grated carrots
½ cup finely chopped celery
¼ cup finely chopped parsley
salad greens

## Beet and Carrot Gelatin

Sprinkle gelatin over the cold water in a small heat-resistant cup and let stand 5 minutes to soften. Place cup in a pan of hot (140°F.) water, stirring until gelatin is dissolved.

In a large mixing bowl, combine lemon juice, beet juice, and yogurt with the dissolved gelatin; beat until thoroughly mixed. Chill until mixture is slightly thickened, stirring occasionally.

*[continued on next page]*

Fold in carrots, celery, and parsley. Lightly oil a 6-cup mold and turn the gelatin mixture into it.

Chill until set, about 6 hours. Unmold and serve with salad greens.

**Yield: 6 servings**

*Variation: To use as a main course, serve with cottage cheese.*

---

1 envelope (1 tablespoon) unflavored gelatin
1 cup milk, divided
2 cups cottage cheese
¼ cup finely chopped (tender part) green onions

1 teaspoon finely minced garlic cloves
2 tablespoons lemon juice
1 cup chopped carrot tops
1 9-inch piecrust
carrot curls for garnish

## Carrot Top and Garlic Pie Filling

Sprinkle gelatin over ¼ cup milk in a small heat-resistant cup and let stand 5 minutes to soften. Place cup in a pan of hot (140°F.) water, stirring until gelatin is dissolved.

Combine remaining milk with cottage cheese in an electric blender. Add dissolved gelatin, onions, garlic, and lemon juice and process until well mixed. Mix in carrot tops.

Turn into the piecrust and decorate with carrot curls placed around the edges. Chill until set.

**Yield: 6 servings**

---

1 envelope (1 tablespoon) plus 1 teaspoon unflavored gelatin
¼ cup cold water

1¼ cups celery juice
1 cup plain yogurt
1 cup finely chopped celery
1 9-inch piecrust

## Celery-Yogurt Pie

Sprinkle gelatin over the cold water in a small heat-resistant cup and let stand 5 minutes to soften. Place cup in a pan of hot (140°F.)

water, stirring until gelatin is dissolved. Cool slightly and stir into the celery juice.

Chill mixture in the refrigerator until it forms a mound when dropped from a spoon.

Add yogurt to the slightly thickened gelatin and beat with a rotary beater just until combined. Stir in celery. Turn filling into the piecrust and refrigerate until set, about 4 hours.

Serve cold.

*Yield: 6 servings*

2 envelopes (2 tablespoons) unflavored gelatin
½ cup cold water
1½ cups milk
2 cups ricotta or cottage cheese
½ cup crumbled blue cheese

¼ cup chopped parsley
1 tablespoon grated onions
½ cup finely chopped green peppers
1 cup chopped tomatoes
½ cup corn kernels

## Confetti Cheese Mold

Lightly grease a 6-cup mold with oil.

Sprinkle gelatin over the cold water in a small heat-resistant cup and let stand 5 minutes to soften. Place cup in a pan of hot (140°F.) water, stirring until gelatin is dissolved.

In a large mixing bowl, beat milk with ricotta and blue cheese until thoroughly combined. Beat in dissolved gelatin.

Chill, stirring occasionally, until mixture mounds when dropped from a spoon. Fold in remaining ingredients. Turn into the prepared mold and chill until firm, preferably overnight.

Unmold before serving.

*Yield: 6 servings*

½ cup raisins or chopped dried apricots
1½ cups Applesauce (see Index)
1 envelope (1 tablespoon) plus 1 teaspoon unflavored gelatin

⅓ cup apple juice
3 cups cottage cheese
1 cup sunflower seeds
1 cup alfalfa sprouts

## Cottage-Applesauce Mold

Soak dried fruit in the applesauce while preparing the other ingredients. Sprinkle gelatin over the apple juice in a small heat-resistant cup and let stand 5 minutes to soften. Place cup in a pan of hot (140°F.) water, stirring until gelatin is dissolved.

Add dissolved gelatin to applesauce and stir until well mixed. Stir in cottage cheese and then sunflower seeds. Turn into a 6-cup mold which has been lightly oiled. Cover and chill until set, about 7 hours.

Unmold gelatin before serving and sprinkle with sprouts.

**Yield: 6 servings**

---

2 tablespoons lemon or lime juice
2 tablespoons cold water
1 envelope (1 tablespoon) unflavored gelatin
1 cup cottage cheese

1 cup plain yogurt
½ pound chopped spinach, stems removed
1 chopped (white part) leek
½ teaspoon curry powder
1 9-inch piecrust

## Cottage-Spinach Pie Filling

Combine lemon juice and water in a small heat-resistant cup and sprinkle gelatin over it. Let stand 5 minutes to soften. Place cup in a pan of hot (140°F.) water, stirring until mixture dissolves.

Process cottage cheese and yogurt in an electric blender until smooth. Add dissolved gelatin and process until thoroughly mixed. Add spinach, leeks, and curry powder to mixture and process until well blended.

Turn into the piecrust and chill until set.

**Yield: 6 servings**

1/4 cup cold water
1 tablespoon cider vinegar
1 envelope (1 tablespoon)
plus 1 teaspoon
unflavored gelatin
1/2 pound tofu
2 cups plain yogurt
1/4 cup chopped dill

3 thinly sliced green onions
1/2 cup chopped black
walnuts
1 cup sliced button
mushrooms
1 cup sliced young green
beans
tomato wedges (optional)

## Dilled Vegetable Mold

Combine cold water and vinegar in a small heat-resistant cup. Sprinkle gelatin over water-vinegar mixture and let stand 5 minutes to soften. Place in a pan of hot (140°F.) water, stirring until gelatin is dissolved.

Process tofu, yogurt, dill, and onions in an electric blender. Add dissolved gelatin and process until mixed.

Transfer to a mixing bowl and thoroughly combine with walnuts, mushrooms, and beans.

Turn into a lightly oiled 6-cup mold and chill until firm. Unmold before serving. If desired, garnish with tomato wedges.

**Yield: 6 servings**

---

2 envelopes (2 tablespoons)
unflavored gelatin
1/2 cup cold water
3 cups pineapple juice

3 egg yolks
1 cup shredded carrots
Nut Cheese Stuffing

## Egg and Carrot Gelatin
## Stuffed with Nut Cheese

Sprinkle gelatin over the water in a small heat-resistant cup and let stand 5 minutes to soften. Place cup in a pan of hot (140°F.) water, stirring until gelatin is dissolved.

[continued on next page]

Combine dissolved gelatin with pineapple juice and egg yolks and beat with a rotary mixer until thoroughly combined.

Chill in the refrigerator until slightly thickened or mixture forms a mound when dropped from a spoon (about 15 minutes). Stir in carrots.

Rinse a 5-cup mold with cold water and fill it with mixture. Chill until set, about 6 hours.

Unmold gelatin and fill ring with the stuffing mixture. Additional stuffing may be heaped in small mounds around the sides of the mold.

*Yield: 6 servings*

---

| | |
|---|---|
| 3 cups cottage cheese | 1 cup chopped black |
| 1 cup chopped green | walnuts (or any other |
| peppers | nuts) |
| 1 cup chopped red sweet | |
| peppers | |

## Nut Cheese Stuffing

Combine all ingredients.

*Yield: about 5 cups*

---

| | |
|---|---|
| 1 envelope (1 tablespoon) | 2 tablespoons lemon juice |
| plus 1 teaspoon | 1 peeled, finely minced |
| unflavored gelatin | shallot |
| ½ cup cold milk | ½ cup chopped parsley |
| ½-¾ cup crumbled blue | 1 cup chopped young green |
| cheese | beans |
| 2 cups plain yogurt | 1 cup chopped black walnuts |

## Gelled Blue Cheese and Green Vegetables

Sprinkle gelatin over the milk in a small heat-resistant cup and let stand 5 minutes to soften. Place cup in a pan of hot (140°F.) water, stirring until gelatin is dissolved.

Beat blue cheese with yogurt and lemon juice until thoroughly mixed. Beat in dissolved gelatin.

Chill until mixture forms a mound when dropped from a spoon.

Fold in remaining ingredients. Turn into an oiled 6-cup mold and chill until firm, preferably overnight. Unmold before serving.

*Yield: 5   1-cup servings*

---

2 envelopes (2 tablespoons)
  unflavored gelatin
½ cup cold water
3½ cups tomato juice
2 tablespoons lemon juice
3 tablespoons chopped
chives or green onions
6 large green peppers
1 head bite-size lettuce
1 head bite-size romaine

1 cup shredded red
  cabbage
1 cup soybean sprouts
2 peeled, diced cucumbers
¼ pound crumbled feta
  cheese
½ cup Zesty Italian Herb
  Dressing (see Index)
6 lemon slices, cut to the
  center on 1 side and then twisted

# Tomato Madrilene in Pepper Cups

Sprinkle gelatin over the water in a small heat-resistant cup and let stand 5 minutes to soften. Place cup in a pan of hot (140°F.) water, stirring until gelatin is dissolved.

In a mixing bowl, combine juices with dissolved gelatin. Chill until nearly set; then stir in chives.

Slice the ends off peppers, remove seeds, wash, and drain upside down in the refrigerator. Spoon chilled mixture into pepper cups and return to refrigerator to chill until gelatin sets.

In a large mixing bowl, combine remaining ingredients and toss lightly to coat with dressing.

Place mixture in salad bowls. Stand a filled pepper cup in the center of each dressed salad. Garnish with a lemon twist.

*Yield: 6 servings*

5 cups plain yogurt
¾ cup half-and-half
2 teaspoons curry powder
¾ cup water
3 envelopes (3 tablespoons)
unflavored gelatin
1 chopped cucumber

1 chopped zucchini
3 thinly sliced green onions
2 chopped tomatoes
½ cup raisins
1 potato
¼ cup chopped dill

## Yogurt-Vegetable Gelatin

Whisk yogurt and half-and-half until thoroughly mixed.

Dissolve curry powder in a ¼ cup water in a heat-resistant bowl. Add remaining ½ cup water. Sprinkle gelatin over the top and let stand 5 minutes to soften. Place bowl in a pan of hot (140°F.) water and stir until gelatin is dissolved.

A little at a time, whisk this mixture into the yogurt mixture and chill until slightly thickened or until mixture forms a mound when dropped from a spoon.

Fold in cucumber, zucchini, green onions, tomatoes, raisins, potato, and dill. Lightly oil a 7-cup mold and turn mixture into it.

Chill until set, about 8 hours. Unmold before serving.

**Yield: 6 servings**

# V. Grains and Seeds

## How to Prepare
## Soaked Whole Grains

Measure out desired amount of grain. Place in a strainer and rinse thoroughly with cold water. Chop coarsely, just enough to break the grains. Transfer to a container and add an equal amount of water — 1 cup grain requires 1 cup water.

Cover the soaking grain with a piece of aluminum foil. Not only will this keep your mixture dust-free, but it will also keep your house pest-free, as fruit flies tend to appear out of nowhere if these mixtures are left uncovered.

The mixture should soak at room temperature 18-24 hours. An 18-hour soaking will yield a chewy texture; a 24-hour soaking will yield a softer texture similar to that of cooked rice.

The grain will absorb all or most of the liquid. Strain it after soaking to remove any excess water. The grain will double in size so that 1 cup dry grain will yield about 2 cups soaked grain.

While soaking, it is possible that your grain will begin to sprout, but this is normal. If soaked longer than 24 hours, the grain will rapidly begin to ferment and may become unpalatable. Do not put soaking grain in the refrigerator, as the cold will inhibit the absorption process. After 18-24 hours, place the soaked, strained grain in a covered container in the refrigerator to slow down this fermentation process. The soaked grain will keep for several days in the refrigerator.

Fruit and vegetable juices are not readily absorbed by whole grains, even when soaked at room temperature. In some cases, depending on the kind of juice used, a rapid fermentation process will result if the two are combined. As an example, if apple juice and wheat are left to soak overnight, the grain will not absorb the juice, but instead will become a bubbly, gaseous mixture. All the recipes using soaked grains in this book require that the grain be soaked in water.

6 cups chopped alfalfa
sprouts
1½ cups ground sunflower
seeds
3 tablespoons finely
chopped onions

3 tablespoons finely
chopped parsley
¾ teaspoon kelp
Herbed Tomato Dressing
(see Index)

## Alfalfa Burgers

Combine ingredients and form into patties.
Top with dressing.

*Yield: 6 servings*

---

1½ cups buckwheat groats
(see Index)
2 cups tomato juice
1 cup plain yogurt
3 thinly sliced green onions
1 finely minced shallot

1 cup chopped celery
1 cup chopped green
peppers
1 cup soybean sprouts
1 head romaine lettuce or
Swiss chard leaves

## Buckwheat Groats Salad

Soak groats in tomato juice about 30 minutes or until liquid is absorbed.

Stir in yogurt, mixing well. Add onions, shallots, celery, peppers, and
sprouts, tossing until combined.

Serve mixture on 6 individual beds of salad greens.

*Yield: 6 servings*

4 cups cottage cheese
2½ cups soaked grain (see Index)
2 cups thinly sliced okra
½ cup chopped parsley
Curried Papaya Dressing
1½ cups alfalfa sprouts

## Cottage Cheese and Grains with Curried Papaya Dressing

Combine cheese, grain, okra, and parsley in a large bowl. Divide mixture among 6 serving plates and form a well in the center of each mound.

Spoon dressing into each well and sprinkle with sprouts.

*Yield: 6 servings*

3 chopped papayas
1 cup orange juice
¼ cup lemon juice
¾ cup oil
1 tablespoon curry powder (optional)

## Curried Papaya Dressing

Process ingredients in an electric blender until smooth.

*Yield: about 4½ cups*

1 pound coarsely mashed tofu
1 cups soaked rye (see Index)
3 thinly sliced green onions
2 tablespoons minced parsley
2 seeded green peppers (1 chopped and 1 cut into 6 rings)
Oil and Vinegar Dressing (see recipe below)
6 lettuce leaves

## Curried Rye and Tofu

Mix the first 4 ingredients with chopped peppers. Add dressing and toss until blended. Cover and refrigerate several hours.

Place a mound on each lettuce leaf and garnish with a pepper ring.

*Yield: 6 servings*

⅓ cup oil
⅓ cup rice vinegar
1 teaspoon curry powder

1 peeled, minced garlic
   clove

## Oil and Vinegar Dressing

Place ingredients in a jar with a lid; cover and shake well to mix. May be prepared a day in advance.

*Yield: about 1 cup*

---

1 small (½ pound) diced
   eggplant
⅓ cup rice or wine vinegar
1 small chopped red onion
1 finely minced garlic clove
2 tablespoons chopped basil
1 pound sliced mushrooms

1 large seeded, chopped
   green pepper
3 cups soaked grain (see
   Index)
2 bunches watercress
Cheddar Dressing

## Eggplant and Grain Salad with Cheddar Dressing

Marinate eggplant with vinegar, onions, garlic, and basil 2–3 hours. Toss with mushrooms, peppers, and grain.

Prepare 6 watercress beds and place a mound of salad on each bed. Top with dressing.

*Yield: 6 servings*

---

1 cup room temperature
   grated cheddar cheese

1 cup plain yogurt
¼ cup rice or wine vinegar

## Cheddar Dressing

Whisk ingredients in a bowl.

*Yield: 2 cups*

2 cups soaked grain (see Index)
⅔ cup coarsely chopped almonds
⅓ cup corn kernels
⅓ cup young peas
⅔ cup chopped green peppers
3 thinly sliced green onions
½ large chopped tomato
Creamy Dressing
1 head romaine lettuce

# Grain and Almond Salad with Creamy Dressing

Combine the first 7 ingredients.
Toss with dressing and serve on romaine leaves.

**Yield: 6 servings**

---

1 cup plain yogurt
½ cup mayonnaise
2 crushed garlic cloves
1 tablespoon lime juice
2 tablespoons oil
1 teaspoon ground cumin
pinch turmeric

## Creamy Dressing

Combine ingredients and chill, covered, overnight in the refrigerator.

**Yield: 1½ cups**

---

3 cups soaked grain (see Index)
3 chopped cucumbers
¼ pound sliced green beans
6 thinly sliced green onions
lettuce leaves
Parsley Sauce

# Grain Salad with Parsley Sauce

Combine grain, cucumbers, beans, and onions in a mixing bowl. Arrange lettuce on serving plates. Mound mixture on beds. Serve with sauce on the side.

**Yield: 6 servings**

1½ cups (tightly packed) finely chopped parsley
⅓ cup rice or cider vinegar
⅔ cup oil

½ cup whole almonds, soaked overnight, then chopped

## Parsley Sauce

Process ingredients in an electric blender until smooth.

**Yield: 2½ cups**

---

3 cups soaked wheat (see Index)
3 chopped tomatoes
1 seeded, chopped green pepper

1 chopped red onion
Zesty Italian Herb Dressing (see Index)
freshly grated Parmesan cheese

## Italian Vegetable Wheat

Combine wheat, tomatoes, peppers, and onions. Spoon mixture into large bowls.

Serve with dressing and top with cheese.

**Yield: 6 servings**

---

1 cup bulgur (see Index)
1 cup rye flakes
½ cup oat flakes
1 juiced lemon
¼ teaspoon minced ginger
1-2 teaspoons coriander to taste
1 teaspoon nutmeg
½ teaspoon cayenne pepper

1 grated carrot
¼ head grated purple cabbage
1 small finely chopped onion
1 finely chopped celery stalk
4 teaspoons ground sesame seeds
6 lettuce leaves
lemon slices for garnish

## Lettuce Rolls

Mix bulgur, rye, oats, and seasonings in a large bowl. Add just enough water to cover. Allow mixture to soak overnight.

The next morning add carrots, cabbage, onions, celery, and seeds. Add enough additional water to make a paste.

Roll up in lettuce leaves like an eggroll. Serve with lemon slices.

**Yield: 6 servings**

3 cups buckwheat groats
(see Index)
2 cups carrot juice
12 thinly sliced green
onions
2 large chopped tomatoes
½ cup finely chopped parsley

½ cup finely chopped mint
1 cup plain yogurt
½ cup mayonnaise
¼ cup lime juice
1 teaspoon curry powder
1 head romaine lettuce

## Middle Eastern Buckwheat Groats

Rinse groats and soak them in carrot juice about 30 minutes or until the juice is absorbed. Mix in the next 4 ingredients.

In a separate bowl, combine yogurt, mayonnaise, lime juice, and curry.

Toss dressing with salad until mixed. Serve on romaine beds.

**Yield: 6 servings**

---

3 cups soaked wheat (see
Index)
1 cup minced green
peppers
3 tablespoons finely
chopped green onions
¼ cup finely chopped radishes
½ cup finely chopped celery

1 peeled, finely minced
garlic clove
½ teaspoon ground nutmeg
1 tablespoon curry powder
⅛ teaspoon ground cloves
⅓ cup mayonnaise
radish roses for garnish

## Molded Wheat

Combine the first 6 ingredients in a large bowl.

Blend nutmeg, curry, and cloves with mayonnaise and taste for seasoning. Thoroughly mix with wheat mixture.

Firmly pack into a lightly oiled 6-cup mold and refrigerate, covered, at least 3–4 hours.

Unmold before serving. Garnish with radish roses.

**Yield: 6 servings**

6 large Italian sweet
   peppers
1 cup grated butternut
   squash
1 cup chopped celery

1 cup soaked grain (see
   Index)
½ pound grated cheddar
   cheese

## Open-Face
## Winter Stuffed Peppers

Remove stems from peppers and cut each in half the long way. Remove insides and discard them. Wash the pepper halves and drain on paper towels.

Combine squash, celery, and grain. Place ¼ cup filling in each pepper half. Sprinkle with cheese.

Serve with your favorite dressing.

**Yield: 6 servings**

---

2 pounds large button
   mushrooms
1½ pounds tofu
3 ounces crumbled blue
   cheese
1 cup soaked grain (see
   Index)
½ cup pomegranate seeds,
   divided

1 cup crushed black
   walnuts
⅓ cup finely chopped
   onions
¼ cup seeded, finely
   chopped green peppers
2 tablespoons oil
1 shredded head lettuce

## Pomegranate-Stuffed
## Mushrooms on Tofu Bed

Chop mushroom stems and set aside. Pat tofu dry with paper towels and mash it with a fork in a medium-size bowl. Blend blue cheese with tofu. Add the grain, mushroom stems, and ¼ cup pomegranate seeds. Divide mixture into 6 portions and shape into flat patties.

In a separate bowl, combine walnuts, onions, peppers, and oil and mix well. Stir in remaining pomegranate seeds. Stuff the button mushrooms with this filling.

Sprinkle each tofu pattie with shredded lettuce. Place stuffed mushrooms atop tofu-lettuce beds.

*Yield: 6 servings*

<table>
<tr><td>

2  pounds thin asparagus<br>    stalks<br>10  thinly sliced radishes<br>1  cubed avocado<br>1  cup Zesty Italian Herb<br>    Dressing (see Index)

</td><td>

</td><td>

2½  cups soaked grain (see Index)<br>1  large finely chopped red<br>    onion<br>1  head lettuce<br>3  tablespoons finely<br>    chopped parsley

</td></tr>
</table>

## Red and Green Vegetables on Grain Beds

Snap off tough ends of asparagus. Cut off tips and slice stalks on the bias into ½-inch pieces. Cut radish slices into julienne strips. Mix avocado cubes with ½ cup dressing in a large mixing bowl to prevent it from discoloring. Add asparagus tips and slices and radish strips, tossing lightly.

Combine grain with the onions in a separate bowl. Toss lightly with remaining dressing.

Arrange lettuce leaves on 6 plates. Place a mound of dressed grain in the center of each lettuce arrangement. Spread center of each mound to form a wide well. Spoon vegetable mixture into wells and sprinkle with parsley.

*Yield: 6 servings*

1 head cauliflower florets
3 sliced zucchini
1 pound quartered button
   mushrooms
Dressing Marinade (see
   recipe below)

2½ cups soaked rye (see Index)
1½ cups shredded or
   grated beets
6 thinly sliced green onions
½ cup chopped celery
2 beaten egg yolks

# Rye Grain with Marinated Vegetables

Combine cauliflower, zucchini, and mushrooms. Cover with dressing and marinate overnight in the refrigerator.

Combine rye, beets, onions, and celery.

Drain off the liquid from marinated vegetables. Beat marinade with egg yolks and pour dressing over the rye mixture, tossing until well mixed.

Place a portion of rye mixture on each plate and form a well in the center of each mound. Fill well with marinated vegetables.

Serve cold.

**Yield: 6 servings**

¼ cup lemon juice
¾ cup oil
1 tablespoon minced chives
1 teaspoon minced chervil
¼ cup minced parsley

1 peeled, finely minced
   garlic clove
¼ teaspoon cayenne
   pepper

## Dressing Marinade

Combine ingredients and mix well.

**Yield: about 1 cup**

3 envelopes (3 tablespoons)
unflavored gelatin
½ cup cold water
¼ cup lemon juice

3 cups tomato juice
1¾ cups orange juice
Grain Stuffing (see recipe
below)

## Stuffed Citrus Aspic Ring

In a small heat-resistant cup, sprinkle gelatin over the water and lemon juice combined and let stand 5 minutes to soften. Place cup in a pan of hot (140°F.) water, stirring until gelatin is dissolved. Combine gelatin with tomato and orange juice.

Rinse a 6-cup ring mold with cold water and fill with gelatin mixture. Chill in the refrigerator until set, about 8 hours or overnight.

**Yield: 6 servings**

---

2½ cups soaked grain (see
Index)
1 cup shredded beets
1 chopped cucumber

3 finely minced shallots
¼ cup chopped parsley
1 large seeded, chopped
green pepper

## Grain Stuffing

Combine ingredients in a large bowl and toss with your favorite dressing.

Unmold citrus aspic and fill the center with stuffing. Any additional stuffing should be placed around the sides of the mold.

**Yield: 6 servings**

1 cup finely shredded
cabbage
1 cup grated carrots
1 cup bean sprouts
1 cup chopped cucumbers
2 cups thinly sliced green
beans

½ cup minced parsley
¼ cup minced chives
3 cups soaked wheat (see
Index)
Sweet and Sour Dressing
(see recipe below)
6 egg yolks

## Sweet and Sour Wheat

Combine all ingredients but dressing and egg yolks in a large bowl. Toss with dressing.

Place a 2-cup mound on each plate and make an indentation in the top of each mound. Place an egg yolk in each indentation.

**Yield: 6 servings**

---

1 tablespoon honey
⅓ cup rice vinegar
2 tablespoons lime juice
3 peeled, finely minced
garlic cloves

1 teaspoon ground ginger
1 teaspoon crushed hot red
peppers
2 teaspoons turmeric

## Sweet and Sour Dressing

Combine ingredients and mix well.

**Yield: about ½ cup**

---

1 cup triticale (see Index)
½ cup millet
½ cup pumpkin seeds
½ cup almonds
½ cup pecans
3½ cups water
1 cup sunflower seeds
½ cup chopped mint

¾ cup chopped parsley
2 minced garlic cloves
6 thinly sliced green onions
6 sliced celery stalks
3 large grated carrots
6 whole egg yolks
lemon wedges for garnish

## Tabouli

In a medium-size bowl, soak triticale, millet, pumpkin seeds, almonds, and pecans in the water, covered, at room temperature 18-24 hours. Strain to remove any liquid that has not been absorbed.

In a large mixing bowl, combine soaked mixture with the next 7 ingredients.

Divide mixture equally among 6 serving plates. Top each mound with a raw egg yolk and garnish with lemon wedges. Serve immediately.

**Yield: 6 servings**

---

1½ pounds tofu
2 ounces crumbled blue cheese
1½ cups soaked wheat or rye (see Index)
1 cup sunflower seeds
¼ cup finely chopped parsley

¼ cup snipped chives
3 cups chopped young green beans
3 cups shredded carrots
3 cups shredded spinach
6 cherry tomatoes

## Tofu Kaleidoscope

Pat the tofu dry with paper towels. Combine tofu and blue cheese and work with fingers until coarsely mashed. Add wheat and sunflower seeds to mixture; then add parsley and chives. Using your hands, toss lightly but thoroughly.

Divide mixture into 6 portions and place on dinner plates. Pat it down to form a neat circle ¼ inch thick.

Starting at the edge and leaving a border of ½ inch, sprinkle ½ cup green beans in a 1-inch strip around each patty. Follow with a circle of ½ cup carrots next to the green beans, then the spinach next to the carrots. Place a cherry tomato in each center.

Serve immediately with your favorite dressing.

**Yield: 6 servings**

6 large tomatoes
2 cups soaked wheat (see
Index)
¼ cup chopped parsley
¼ cup finely chopped
celery

2 tablespoons finely
chopped basil
2 ounces mashed blue
cheese
¼ cup mayonnaise

## Tomatoes Stuffed with Wheat

Slice tops off the tomatoes and set them aside. Using a spoon, scoop out the insides. Turn hollowed tomatoes upside down on paper towels to drain.

In a mixing bowl, combine remaining ingredients. Fill each tomato with mixture. Replace tops. Serve immediately.

*Yield: 6 servings*

3 cups soaked grain (see
Index)
2 cups chopped celery
1 cup chopped black
walnuts

⅔ cup raisins
mayonnaise
3 large red apples
½ juiced lemon
6 beds lettuce

## Waldorf Grain Entree

Combine grain with celery, walnuts, and raisins. Toss mixture with enough mayonnaise to coat.

Dice apples directly into a bowl containing lemon juice and enough cold water to cover. Drain and dry the apples and stir them into mixture.

To serve, place a mound on each lettuce bed.

*Yield: 6 servings*

2 pounds halved lengthwise
   zucchini
¼ cup lemon juice
1 cup oil
2 finely minced garlic
   cloves
2 cups soaked grain (see
   Index)

½ cup sliced radishes
½ cup chopped green
   peppers
3 thinly sliced (tender part)
   green onions

## Zucchini and Grain

Cut zucchini halves into thin slices.

Place lemon juice in a large salad bowl and gradually whisk in the oil until well combined. Beat in garlic.

Add zucchini and remaining ingredients, tossing until well coated with dressing. Serve chilled.

**Yield: 6 servings**

# VI. Meat

1 pound eye of the round
1 medium carrot
1 tablespoon grated onions
⅓ cup olive oil

coarsely ground pepper to
   taste
1 small quartered lemon
4 stalks celery

## Beef Parchment

Freeze beef. Remove from freezer about 1 hour before beginning preparation. When partially defrosted, slice beef paper thin.

Scrape carrot. With a vegetable slicer, cut very thin carrot curls lengthwise.

Mix onions and oil.

With paper towels, blot excess moisture from meat. Arrange on individual plates and top with drizzling of oil-onion mixture.

Arrange carrot curls on top. Pepper to taste and garnish with lemon and celery. Serve immediately.

**Yield: 4 appetizers or 2 main servings**

2 pounds ground very lean
  beef, veal, or lamb
4 teaspoons green peppers
½ cup finely minced
  onions

4 teaspoons finely chopped
  parsley
freshly ground black pepper
  to taste
6 egg yolks for garnish

## Beef, Veal, or Lamb Tartare

Combine meat, green peppers, onions, and parsley in a mixing bowl. Add pepper to taste.

Divide into 6 portions and shape into patties. Make a small well in the center of each patty and top with an egg yolk.

**Yield: 6 servings**

*Variation: Cheeseburgers*
Sprinkle each patty with freshly grated cheddar cheese.

*Variation: Blue Cheeseburgers*
Sprinkle each patty with crumbled blue cheese. Then top with egg yolk and sprinkle with alfalfa sprouts.

---

1 cup alfalfa sprouts
12 long, thin slices lean
  beef, filet mignon
(tenderloin) if possible

36 asparagus tips
12 sliced button mushrooms

## Beef with Sprouts and Asparagus Tips

Sprinkle sprouts over 1 side of each beef slice. Wrap 3 asparagus tips in each slice of sprinkled beef.

Place overlapping mushrooms on top of each beef roll.

**Yield: 6 servings**

*Variation: An equal amount of whole young green beans may be substituted for asparagus tips.*

| | |
|---|---|
| 2 tablespoons tamari soy sauce | 1½ pounds ¾-inch cubes filet mignon (tenderloin) |
| 2 tablespoons lime juice | 12 cherry tomatoes |
| 4 finely minced shallots | 12 skinned pearl onions |
| 1 teaspoon honey | 12 button mushrooms |
| 1 teaspoon ginger | Peanut Dressing (see Index) |

## Indonesian-Style Meat Kebabs

Combine the soy sauce, lime juice, shallots, honey, and ginger, mixing well. Add beef cubes and toss to coat evenly.

Cover and marinate in the refrigerator 4 hours.

Place beef, tomatoes, onions, and mushrooms in an alternating pattern on 12 skewers.

Serve with dressing.

**Yield: 6 servings**

---

| | |
|---|---|
| 2 pounds ground lean lamb | ¼ cup chopped chives |
| 3 finely minced shallots | 2 pounds okra |
| ½ cup finely chopped parsley | 6 egg yolks |

## Lamb Tartare with Okra

Combine lamb, shallots, parsley, and chives, mixing thoroughly. Shape into 12 slightly flattened patties.

Remove stem ends from okra and divide it into 6 equal piles. Place 1 pile of okra, cutsides facing outward, around the top of 6 patties. Sandwich okra patties with the remaining 6 patties.

Place egg yolk atop each patty. Serve immediately.

**Yield: 6 servings**

1½ pounds ground very lean beef
1 cup soaked grain (see Index)
3 finely minced shallots
¾ cup minced parsley

3 thinly sliced green onions
1 lightly beaten egg yolk
18 large Bib or Boston lettuce leaves
6 shredded carrots for garnish

## Lettuce Rolls Stuffed with Beef and Grain

Combine beef, grain, shallots, parsley, onions, and egg yolk, mixing well. Place a portion of mixture in the center of each lettuce leaf.

Fold the base of the leaf over the filling, then the sides, and finally the top edge. Place seamside down on a serving plate or individual dishes and surround with shredded carrots.

**Yield: 6 servings**

---

1½ pounds lean beef
1½ cups oil
½ cup lemon juice
1 teaspoon oregano
½ teaspoon basil

1 minced garlic clove
¾ pound sliced lengthwise mushrooms
½ head lettuce
parsley sprigs for garnish

## Marinated Mushrooms and Steak Slivers

Freeze beef. About 1 hour before preparation time, remove from freezer. Thinly slice partially frozen beef.

In a medium-size bowl, combine oil, juice, oregano, basil, and garlic.

Place beef and mushroom slices in a flat glass dish. Pour marinade over. Gently mix and refrigerate 2 hours, stirring after 1 hour.

Drain off marinade. Serve beef and mushrooms on a large platter surrounded by lettuce and garnished with parsley.

**Yield: 6 servings**

1½ pounds ground very lean beef, veal, or lamb  
1 lightly beaten egg yolk  
1 small finely chopped onion  
2 tablespoons minced mint leaves  

½ teaspoon freshly grated nutmeg  
12 cashews  
1 cup minced parsley  

## Meatball Surprise

Combine the meat, egg yolk, onions, mint, and nutmeg in a mixing bowl.

Shape into 12 meatballs. Place a cashew in the center of each ball and smooth it over.

Sprinkle with parsley.

**Yield: 6 servings**

---

1½ pounds finely ground very lean lamb  
½ pound finely ground very lean beef  
¼ cup finely chopped onions  
¼ cup plain yogurt  
¼ teaspoon cayenne pepper  

½ pound rinsed, crumbled feta cheese  
1 large finely chopped sweet red pepper  
¼ cup minced mint leaves  
½ cup minced parsley  
2 lemons cut into thirds for garnish  

## Middle Eastern Meat Loaf

In a large mixing bowl, combine lamb, beef, onions, yogurt, and cayenne pepper. Divide mixture in half.

On a serving platter, shape half meat mixture into a loaf about 1 inch high.

Sprinkle loaf with cheese and then with red peppers. Combine mint and parsley. Sprinkle half this mixture over peppers.

Shape remaining meat mixture into a similar-size loaf and place it atop the first so that cheese is in the center.

Sprinkle the top with remaining mint-parsley mixture. Garnish with lemon wedges around the base of loaf.

**Yield: 6 servings**

1 pound very thinly sliced
filet mignon (tenderloin)
12 slices Swiss cheese

½ teaspoon dry mustard
¼ cup mayonnaise
6 thinly sliced green onions

## Steak and Cheese Sandwich

Lay meat evenly on 6 slices of cheese.

Combine mustard with mayonnaise. Spread a little of this mixture over meat. Sprinkle with onions and top with remaining cheese slices. Cut each sandwich in half or quarters before serving.

**Yield: 6 servings**

---

1 pound finely ground lean
veal
¼ cup finely ground
almonds

2 tablespoons plain yogurt
2 tablespoons finely minced
parsley
3 thinly sliced green onions

## Stuffed Veal
## and Almond Rolls

In a mixing bowl, combine veal, almonds, yogurt, and parsley.

Brush a large cutting board with cold water. Pat veal mixture down into a square shape. Cover with a large piece of wax paper.

Using a rolling pin, roll it into a 12-inch square. Remove wax paper. Cut veal into 4-inch squares. Sprinkle with onions.

Using a small spatula, roll up each square as if you were making a jelly roll. Cover and chill before serving.

**Yield: 3 servings**

Note: To serve 6, make this recipe twice in 2 separate batches.

# Side Dishes

# Side Dishes

# I. Fruits and Vegetables

2 cups grated Jerusalem
   artichokes
1 cup grated carrots
¼ cup chopped celery
¼ cup olive oil

½ cup lemon juice
½ teaspoon rosemary
1 teaspoon ginger
¼ cup chopped nasturtium
   flowers

## Artichokes and Flowers

In a bowl, combine artichokes, carrots, and celery.

In a cup, mix oil, juice, rosemary, and ginger. Pour over vegetables and toss.

Sprinkle with nasturtium flowers and serve.

*Yield: 6 servings*

---

2 cups thinly sliced
Jerusalem artichokes
½ cup lentil sprouts
½ cup shredded zucchini
1 cup thinly sliced green
   peppers

1 cup sour cream or ½
   pound ricotta cheese
2 teaspoons tamari soy
   sauce
parsley for garnish

## Artichokes in Cream

Combine artichokes, sprouts, zucchini, and peppers in a salad bowl.

In a cup, mix sour cream or ricotta cheese, and soy sauce. Pour dressing over vegetables and toss thoroughly.

Garnish with parsley.

*Yield: 4-6 servings*

2 thinly sliced avocadoes
½ pound thinly sliced
   mushrooms
⅓ cup olive oil
1 juiced lemon

1 tablespoon white wine vinegar
1 tablespoon chopped
   parsley
1 crushed garlic clove
pinch pepper

## Avocadoes and Mushrooms Cosmopolitan

In a shallow bowl, arrange layers of avocadoes and mushrooms.

In a separate bowl, combine oil, lemon juice, vinegar, parsley, garlic, and pepper.

Pour mixture over avocadoes and chill at least 1 hour before serving.

**Yield: 6-8 servings**

---

2 medium peeled, coarsely
   grated beets
½ cup chopped celery

2 tablespoons finely
   chopped onions
½ grated carrot
½ cup plain yogurt

## Beet Salad

Mix ingredients. Chill before serving.

**Yield: 6 servings**

4 cups thinly sliced turnips
1 cup thinly sliced carrots
1 teaspoon tamari soy sauce
½ cup vinegar

1 tablespoon honey
½-1 teaspoon freshly
grated ginger (optional)

## Carrots and Turnips in Vinegar Sauce

Slice turnips and carrots crosswise.

Mix soy sauce, vinegar, and honey and pour over vegetables. Mix thoroughly and chill. Before serving, ginger may be added.

*Yield: 6 servings*

---

1 peeled, thinly sliced
cucumber
2 cups sliced radishes
1 medium thinly sliced onion

ice water
1 cup sour cream
2 tablespoons vinegar

## Cucumbers and Radishes in Sour Cream

Place cucumbers, radishes, and onions in a large bowl. Cover with ice water.

Combine sour cream and vinegar.

To serve, drain vegetables. Stir in sour cream mixture until vegetables are well coated. Serve immediately.

*Yield: 6 servings*

3 cups thinly sliced    ½ cup vinegar
        cucumbers    1½ tablespoons minced dill
2 teaspoons honey    1 minced garlic clove

## Dilled Cucumbers

Place cucumbers in a large bowl.
In a separate bowl, combine remaining ingredients and mix thoroughly. Toss dressing with cucumbers.
Chill before serving.

*Yield: 3 cups*

3 tablespoons lemon juice    ⅔ cup coarsely chopped
¼ teaspoon ground ginger        peanuts
3 ½-inch-cubed avocadoes

## Gingered Avocadoes

In a serving bowl, combine lemon juice and ginger and stir until well mixed. Add avocado cubes and toss gently.
Marinate mixture at least 30 minutes and sprinkle with peanuts.

*Yield: 6 servings*

1 cup oil    1 tablespoon chopped green
⅓ cup red wine vinegar        peppers
1 tablespoon chopped    ½ teaspoon tamari soy
        pimentos        sauce
1 tablespoon chopped    2½ cups green beans
chives or green onions

## Green Beans Vinaigrette

Combine all ingredients but beans in a bottle or jar. Cover and shake well. Place beans in a large bowl and pour dressing over them.
Cover and refrigerate at least 3 hours, stirring occasionally.
Drain before serving.

*Yield: 3⅔ cups*

3 green peppers
1 grated carrot
½ cup grated cabbage
2 chopped tomatoes
2 small diced zucchini
1 chopped green onion
5 diced radishes

1½ tablespoons parsley
½ finely chopped red
  pepper
½ cup chopped broccoli
Yogurt-Cucumber Dressing
  (see Index)
spinach leaves

## Green Pepper Boats

Cut peppers in half lengthwise, remove seeds and membrane, and wash.

Combine chopped vegetables in a bowl. Stir in enough dressing to bind vegetables together well.

Stuff pepper halves with mixture and arrange on a plate covered with spinach leaves.

Chill before serving.

**Yield: 6 servings**

---

4 celery hearts
1 large peeled, wedged
  tomato
⅓ cup olive oil
2 tablespoons lemon juice

½ teaspoon basil
tamari soy sauce to taste
3 tablespoons chopped
  parsley

## Hearts of Celery

Split each celery heart in half lengthwise. Cut out the root and trim the leaves, leaving only the smallest. Cut into 1½-inch pieces, wipe dry, and place in a salad bowl. Add tomato wedges.

Combine oil, juice, basil, and soy sauce; pour over celery and tomato. Mix well.

Top with parsley.

**Yield: 6 servings**

8 cups plain yogurt
1⅓ cups olive oil
½ cup lemon juice
2 finely minced garlic
   cloves
1½ teaspoons minced dill

1½ pounds button
   mushrooms
¾ cup chopped black
   walnuts
1 head romaine lettuce

## Marinated Mushrooms with Yogurt Cheese

Place yogurt in a fine-mesh muslin bag or large square of muslin tied at the ends. Tie bag onto kitchen faucet and suspend over a bowl to catch the drippings; leave overnight at room temperature.

Combine the oil, juice, garlic, and dill in a 1-quart jar. Cover and shake well to mix. Halve mushrooms directly into marinade. Cover and store mixture in the refrigerator overnight.

To serve, remove cheese mixture from bag and blend in nuts. Shape mixture into small balls, about ½ inch in diameter.

Divide romaine among 6 plates; divide balls and place atop romaine. Ladle mushrooms over balls.

Cover and shake marinade to mix. Serve separately to be used as additional dressing.

*Yield: 6 servings*

---

2 cups chopped zucchini or
   eggplant
1 tablespoon chopped green
   onions
1 finely chopped garlic
   clove
1 large chopped tomato
   (optional)

1 tablespoon chopped herbs
   (oregano, basil, dill,
   parsley)
½ cup oil
¼ cup vinegar
1 tablespoon honey

## Marinated Zucchini

Combine vegetables and herbs. Mix oil, vinegar, and honey and pour over salad.

Let stand in the refrigerator at least 1 hour before serving.

*Yield: 4-6 servings*

6 cups coarsely grated parsnips
1 cup chopped celery
3 tablespoons chopped onions or green onions
⅛ teaspoon cayenne pepper

¼ teaspoon dry mustard
¾ minced garlic clove
1½ cups mayonnaise
salad greens
paprika for garnish

## Mock Crabmeat

Combine ingredients and serve on salad greens.
Garnish with paprika.

**Yield: 6 servings**

---

4 cups snow peas
1 cup hickory nuts or pecans

2 tablespoons tamari soy sauce
2 tablespoons olive oil

## Nutty Snow Peas

Combine peas and nuts. Sprinkle with soy sauce and oil.
Mix thoroughly and serve.

**Yield: 6 servings**

---

1 quart shelled peas
1 thinly sliced green onion
½ cup mayonnaise

1 cup sliced mushrooms or chilled cheddar cheese cubes
lettuce leaves

## Pea Salad

Mix peas, onions, and mayonnaise.
Stir in mushrooms or cheese and serve on lettuce.

**Yield: 6 servings**

4½ cups green beans
¾ cup finely chopped
walnuts, almonds, or
peanuts

1½ cups plain yogurt
¾ cup mayonnaise
2 crushed garlic cloves

## Quick Bean Dish

Mix beans and nuts.

In a separate bowl, combine yogurt, mayonnaise, and garlic.

Pour dressing over mixture. Toss lightly and serve.

**Yield: 6 servings**

---

2 cups shredded parsnips
½ cup chopped green
peppers
1 cup grated or finely
chopped carrots
1 peeled, cored, diced
apple

2 tablespoons sour cream
3 tablespoons oil
1 tablespoon cider vinegar
tamari soy sauce to taste
1 small head leafy lettuce
(optional)

## Shredded Parsnips

Combine parsnips, peppers, carrots, and apples in a bowl.

Mix together sour cream, oil, vinegar, and soy sauce. Add to vegetables and toss.

Serve over lettuce leaves if desired.

**Yield: 6 servings**

---

4 coarsely chopped
tomatoes
6 thinly sliced okra pods
2 chopped green onions
½ sliced green pepper
½ teaspoon basil

¼ teaspoon oregano
1 minced garlic clove
¼ cup Parmesan cheese
3 tablespoons lemon juice
sprouts

## Sprouts with Italian Herbs

Place vegetables in a bowl. Mix herbs, garlic, and cheese. Toss these and lemon juice with vegetables.

Serve over a large bowl of sprouts.

**Yield: 6   ½-cup servings**

6 large tomatoes
¼ head chopped lettuce
½ cup chopped spinach
½ cup chopped endive
¼ cup corn kernels
1 shredded carrot

1 stalk chopped celery
1 chopped green pepper
¼ cup sprouts
4 teaspoons caraway seeds
¼ cup sunflower seeds
¼ cup mayonnaise

## Stuffed Tomatoes

Cut the ends off tomatoes and scoop out the insides. Combine chopped vegetables with tomato pulp. Add sprouts and seeds. Mix in mayonnaise.

Fill tomatoes with mixture and cover with your favorite dressing.

**Yield: 6 servings**

---

2 cups corn kernels
1 large diced tomato
2 tablespoons minced onions
2 stalks diced celery

½ cup chopped green peppers
1 minced garlic clove
⅓ cup mayonnaise
pepper and paprika to taste

## Sweet Corn

Combine vegetables. Add mayonnaise and seasonings.

**Yield: 4 cups**

---

2 diced tomatoes
½ cup wheat sprouts
½ cup buckwheat sprouts

2 chopped carrots
1 cup cottage cheese
lettuce leaves

## Tomato-Sprout Salad

Mix together. Serve on lettuce.

**Yield 4-6 servings**

1 sliced cucumber
1 small sliced zucchini
2 sliced tomatoes
½ cup mung sprouts
¼ cup sunflower sprouts or
seeds

1 teaspoon herbs (oregano,
basil, thyme)
2 tablespoons oil
2 tablespoons apple cider
vinegar or lemon juice
1 cup cottage cheese

# Vegetable Medley with Cottage Cheese

Combine all ingredients but cottage cheese.
Make a well in center of salad and put cottage cheese in well.

**Yield: 6 servings**

---

2 cups peanuts, soaked
overnight
2 cups (6 medium) sliced
Jerusalem artichokes
1 small chopped onion
1 teaspoon dill seed

2 teaspoons tamari soy
sauce
parsley and/or dill for
garnish
lettuce leaves

# Winter Reliable

Put peanuts and artichokes through food grinder with finest attachment.
Mix in onions, dill, and soy sauce.
Garnish with parsley and/or dill and serve on lettuce.

**Yield: 4 cups**

---

3 cups alfalfa sprouts
1 cup coarsely grated
carrots

1 cup sunflower seeds
½ cup coarsely chopped
celery

# Winter Vegetables

Mix together and toss with your favorite dressing.

**Yield: 6 servings**

# II. Pickles and Relishes

1 pound unthawed frozen
    cranberries
2 medium unpeeled,
    quartered oranges

2 teaspoons lemon juice
¾ cup honey

## Cranberry Relish

Combine ingredients in a large bowl. Process half in an electric blender until well chopped. Repeat procedure with the balance of ingredients. Mix with the first portion already in the bowl.

Refrigerate 3 days before using.

***Yield: 6-8 servings***

2 cups grated or chopped
    carrots
½ grated or chopped onion
2 tablespoons finely
chopped coriander leaves
    or parsley

1 teaspoon minced ginger
    (or less)
1 small juiced lime or
    lemon

## Fresh Carrot Chutney

Mix ingredients. Let stand at least ½ hour before serving.
Serve well chilled.

***Yield: about 3 cups***

6 medium thinly sliced zucchini
1 chopped green pepper
2-3 sliced green onions with tops

2 teaspoons celery seed
½ cup honey
½ cup lemon juice or ¼ cup cider vinegar
1 thinly sliced, halved lemon

## Fresh Lemon-Zucchini Pickles

Place the first 4 ingredients in a large bowl. Add honey, juice or vinegar, and lemon slices.

Refrigerate overnight in a covered jar.

Keeps well several weeks.

*Yield: 6 servings*

2 cups thin tomato wedges
5 thinly sliced diagonally green onions
1 thinly sliced cucumber
1 cup alfalfa sprouts

1 teaspoon tamari soy sauce
2 tablespoons sesame seeds
2 tablespoons oil
1 minced garlic clove

## Fresh Vegetable Relish

Combine tomatoes, onions, cucumbers, and sprouts in a medium-size bowl.

In a separate bowl, mix soy sauce, sesame seeds, oil, and garlic. Shake well.

Pour over vegetables and serve immediately.

*Yield: 6 servings*

¼ pound mint
1 medium chopped or grated onion
1½ juiced limes

4 tablespoons minced coriander leaves or parsley
cayenne pepper to taste
1 teaspoon honey

## Mint Chutney

Remove mint from stalks. Blend leaves with onions and part of the lime juice. Then add the rest of the ingredients and blend well.

Chill for several hours to let flavors meld. Serve cold.

*Yield: about 1½ cups*

4 cups peeled, sliced
cucumbers
½ cup sliced green peppers
½ cup sliced sweet red
peppers

½ cup sliced onions
1 cup cider vinegar
½ teaspoon celery seed

## Salad Relish

Mix together cucumbers, green peppers, red peppers, and onions.
Add vinegar and celery seed.

Place in a container. Cover and refrigerate. Do not freeze.

Use as needed.

**Yield: 6 servings**

---

3 bunches watercress
3 chopped green onions
and tops
⅛ teaspoon cayenne
pepper

2 teaspoons tamari soy
sauce or to taste
1½ tablespoons vinegar
¼ teaspoon crushed red
pepper
2 teaspoons sesame seeds

## Watercress Relish

Cut watercress into 2-inch lengths and mix together green onions,
cayenne, soy sauce, vinegar, and crushed red pepper. Pour over watercress, then sprinkle with sesame seeds.

Chill or serve at room temperature.

**Yield: 6 servings**

# Dips, Sandwiches, Fillings, and Spreads

# Dips, Sandwiches, Fillings, and Spreads

# I. Dips

2 cups finely chopped spinach
½ cup finely chopped parsley
½ cup finely chopped chives
1 cup sour cream
½ teaspoon minced garlic
2 teaspoons sesame seeds

## Aunt Jane's Green Dip

Mix spinach, parsley, and chives in a medium-size bowl.
Fold in sour cream. Add garlic and sesame seeds and stir well.
Serve with vegetables.

**Yield: 3 cups**

---

1 cup sour cream
⅓ cup loosely packed crumbled blue cheese
½ teaspoon tamari soy sauce

## Blue Cheese Dip

Combine ingredients. Chill to blend flavors.
Serve with apple slices.

**Yield: 1⅓ cups**

---

1 cup cottage cheese
1 cup mayonnaise
1 small grated onion
1 tablespoon tamari soy sauce or to taste
½ teaspoon crushed celery seed
1 crushed garlic clove
chopped parsley and thinly sliced green onions for garnish

## Cottage Dip

Briefly process ingredients in an electric blender.
Pour into a low serving bowl and garnish with parsley and onions.

**Yield: 2 cups**

1 cup plain yogurt or sour cream  
¼ cup mayonnaise  
½ teaspoon celery seeds  

1 tablespoon minced dill  
1 teaspoon minced onions  
1 minced garlic clove  
½ teaspoon horseradish  

## Creamy Dill Dip

Combine ingredients and mix thoroughly. Cover and chill at least 2 hours before serving.

Serve with your favorite vegetables.

*Yield: 1¼ cups*

---

½ cup sour cream  
½ cup mayonnaise  

1 cup finely diced cucumbers  
1 teaspoon lemon juice  

## Cucumber Dip

Combine ingredients thoroughly.  
Chill well before serving.

*Yield: 2 cups*

---

4 cups peeled, diced cucumbers  
3 cups plain yogurt  

2 teaspoons crushed mint leaves  
1 small finely chopped garlic clove  

## Cucumbers with Yogurt and Mint

Mix ingredients thoroughly in a bowl.  
Chill in the refrigerator until serving time.  
Use as a dip for vegetables or as a soup.

*Yield: 6 servings*

½ cup mayonnaise   ¼ teaspoon chili powder
½ cup plain yogurt   ¼ teaspoon ginger
1 teaspoon curry powder   pinch cayenne pepper
½ teaspoon turmeric

## Curry Dip

Place ingredients in a small bowl and mix thoroughly.
Cover and refrigerate 1–2 hours before serving.
Serve in a low bowl with vegetable pieces.

**Yield: 1 cup**

---

1 cup cottage cheese   1 cup pineapple cubes

## Fruit Dip

Process cottage cheese and pineapple in an electric blender until smooth.
Empty mixture into a low bowl and serve as a dip with fruit spears.

**Yield: 2 cups**

---

2 cups plain yogurt   1 chopped green pepper
2 thinly sliced green onions   1 diced cucumber
2 tablespoons chopped   ¼ cup finely chopped
chives   spinach or Swiss chard
1 diced celery stalk   tarragon, summer savory,
1 grated carrot   comfrey, or chili to taste

## Labneh Dip

To make labneh, a yogurt cheese similar to cream cheese, place 2 cups plain yogurt in cheesecloth or a piece of clean old sheet. Form cloth into a bag over the yogurt, and loop it over the kitchen sink faucet so it can drip freely overnight.

The next morning, put labneh in a dish and chill in the refrigerator a few hours.

[continued on next page]

In a separate bowl, combine vegetables and seasoning. Lightly stir vegetables into labneh.

Refrigerate until ready to serve.

**Yield: 4 cups**

6 medium tomatoes  ½ cup jalapeno peppers, or
½ cup minced onions  more, depending on taste

## Mexican Salsa

Chop tomatoes, onions, and peppers. Let stand 1 hour to let flavors blend.

Spoon mixture over vegetables to perk up appetites or just eat from the bowl.

**Yield: 2 cups**

*Note: If you like things mild, use green chilis. Jalapeno peppers are very hot.*

3 cups basil leaves  chopped nuts or seeds to
2 minced garlic cloves  taste if desired
¾ cup oil

## Pesto

Chop basil or process in an electric blender.

Add garlic and oil and mix well. Chopped nuts and seeds can also be added.

Serve immediately over sprouts or as a dip for vegetables.

**Yield: 2 cups**

1 small sliced onion  1 cup plain yogurt
1 crushed garlic clove  ½ teaspoon turmeric
½ sliced cucumber  ½ teaspoon ginger
½ sliced green pepper  ⅛ teaspoon chili powder
2 stalks diced celery  ⅛ teaspoon ground cumin
water

## Vegetable Dip

Place onions, garlic, cucumbers, green peppers, and celery in an electric blender with enough water to cover. Process 10-15 seconds until it reaches a mushy consistency. Squeeze out liquid. Mix this pulp with the remaining ingredients.

Use as a dip for carrot sticks, pepper strips, cucumber slices, cherry tomatoes, or any other vegetable.

*Yield: 1½ cups*

# II. Sandwiches

## Bread Sandwiches

Unbaked breads made with flour are best served in small portions. Smear slices with Homemade Peanut Butter,* Plum Butter,* or cream cheese sweetened with honey and pieces of dried fruit. Serve open face.

## Cheese Sandwiches

Substitute thick slices of cheese for baked bread in making sandwiches. You will need 2 large slices about ⅛ inch thick for each sandwich. Here is a list of some suitable varieties: Swiss, Provolone, Tilsit, Muenster, Cheddar, and Monterey Jack.

Before adding grated vegetables, sprouts, or nuts to these sandwiches, it is best to cover the cheeses with a soft spread of nut butter, cottage or ricotta cheese, or mashed tofu to bind the contents of the sandwiches together. Other fillings that go well with these sandwiches are Ruby Sandwich Filling,* Caraway-Cabbage Sandwich Filling,* and Cress Sandwich Filling.*

## Fruit Sandwiches

Choose firm fruit that does not contain too much juice. Certain types of apples such as Rome, Delicious, and Granny, Seckle pears, and even some firm bananas make good sandwiches.

Cut apples and pears in half lengthwise and core each piece. Cut each half into about 3 slices. Smear slices with a sticky spread such as

*[continued on next page]*

*See Index for recipe.

Date-Apricot Jam,* Crunchy Peanut Butter Spread,* or Cinnamon-Honey Spread.* Scatter the spread with such additions as coconut, chopped or grated nuts, raisins, currants, and sunflower seeds. Top each slice with another piece of fruit of the same shape or serve open face.

## Vegetable Sandwiches

Personal preference will determine the "bread" for your vegetable sandwiches. Most firm vegetables such as zucchini, cucumbers, firm red tomatoes, green tomatoes, and peppers take various spreads, sprouts, and garnishes very well. Slice all vegetables. Place a spiral of carrot peel in the opening of pepper rings. Smear slices with such spreads as Cheddar-Onion Spread,* Mushroom Spread,* nut butters, or cottage cheese. If desired, scatter finely chopped green onions, ground nuts, and sprouts. Top with another slice of the same vegetable or serve open face.

*See Index for recipe.

# III. Sandwich Fillings

## Avocado Sandwich Filling

Mash some avocado with a small amount of lemon juice in a bowl. Mix in a little grated onion, finely chopped tomato, and soaked wheat (see Index).

## Banana Sandwich Filling

Spread cheese slices with peanut butter. Mash some banana with a small amount of lemon juice to prevent it from discoloring. Mix some pomegranate seeds into the mashed banana and spread on the peanut butter.

## Caraway-Cabbage Sandwich Filling

In a bowl, mix some finely shredded red and/or green cabbage with enough mayonnaise to bind. Stir in some caraway seeds and spread mixture on cheese slices.

## Cottage-Potato Sandwich Filling

In a bowl, mix cottage cheese with a little grated onion, minced garlic, chopped chives, and parsley. Grate raw potato directly into the mixture to prevent it from discoloring. Spread on cheese slices.

## Cress Sandwich Filling

In a bowl, combine some cottage cheese with grated cucumber. Spread on cheese slices and top with watercress before closing sandwich.

## Golden Sandwich Filling

In a bowl, combine mashed tofu with some finely chopped golden raisins, shredded carrot or butternut squash, and pine nuts.

## Herb Sandwich Filling

In a bowl, mash some softened cream cheese with chopped chives, chervil, basil, parsley, or dill or a mixture of these. Stir in a little lemon juice and a few spoonfuls of soaked grain (see Index).

## Nutty Sandwich Filling

Combine equal parts of nut butter with mashed tofu. Sprinkle with sprouts.

## Ruby Sandwich Filling

Spread cheese slices with ricotta cheese. Top with a mixture of shredded beets and pomegranate seeds.

## Rye-Ricotta Sandwich Filling

In a bowl, combine ricotta cheese with some chopped basil and parsley. Mix in a few spoonfuls of soaked rye (see Index). Spread on cheese slices.

# IV. Sandwich Spreads

½ cup almonds    ¼ cup mayonnaise
½ cup chopped celery

## Almond-Celery Spread

Grind together almonds and celery and lightly stir in the mayonnaise. If more mayonnaise is desired, add enough to reach a spreadlike consistency. Mix thoroughly.

*Yield: 1 cup*

1 chopped green pepper
1 large chopped celery stalk
1 medium chopped mild onion
1 large chopped carrot
3 cups ground almonds
2 tablespoons tarragon
2 tablespoons ground caraway seeds or 1½ teaspoons crushed caraway seeds

1½ teaspoons ground cumin
1 tablespoon curry powder
½ teaspoon ground cayenne pepper
2 tablespoons tamari soy sauce or to taste

## Almond-Vegetable Spread

Combine vegetables in a large bowl. Mix in remaining ingredients and mix until well blended.

This spread should be about the consistency of peanut butter.

This makes an excellent spread for thick tomato slices or any other vegetable rounds. Or try it rolled up in a leaf.

*Yield: 3 cups*

¾ cup grated cheddar     1 tablespoon finely minced
     cheese          parsley
2 thinly sliced green onions   2 tablespoons mayonnaise

## Cheddar-Onion Spread

Combine cheese, onions, and parsley with just enough mayonnaise to bind.

**Yield: 1 cup**

---

¼ pound butter
½ cup honey                 1 teaspoon cinnamon

## Cinnamon-Honey Spread

Mix ingredients with a spoon until well blended.
Use as a spread on fruit slices.

**Yield: about ⅔ cup**

---

⅔ cup peanut butter     ¼ cup plain yogurt
½ cup shredded carrots   2 tablespoons honey
¼ cup finely chopped     ¼ cup chopped sunflower
    celery         seeds

## Crunchy Peanut Butter Spread

Mix ingredients thoroughly and use as a spread on zucchini rounds, cucumber disks, or apple slices.

**Yield: about 2 cups**

2 cups cold water   1 cup dried apricots
1 cup pitted dates

# Date-Apricot Jam

Process ingredients in an electric blender until smooth. (If you prefer a chewy texture, add apricots last and process only until they reach the desired consistency.)

Serve with fruit or yogurt or smeared on bread.

**Yield: 3 cups**

*Note: Any kind of dried fruit can be substituted for apricots — peaches, figs, pears. Apricots can be soaked in water to soften if desired.*

2½ cups peanuts   ½ teaspoon tamari soy
¼–½ cup peanut oil   sauce or to taste

# Homemade Peanut Butter

In an electric blender, puree peanuts, a few at a time, with oil and soy sauce. If you chooose a crunchier spread, blend the last batches for a shorter period of time.

Store, covered, in the refrigerator.

**Yield: 1¾ cups**

2 cups soybeans   water to cover

# Homemade Raw Tofu

Place soybeans in a container, cover with water, and allow to soak overnight (12 hours). Drain and refrigerate liquid. Allow soybeans to sprout 36 hours, rinsing and draining well every 8 hours. (Discard this liquid.)

Place about 1 cup sprouted beans in an electric blender, gradually adding reserved liquid as you process to make a thick creamy consistency, the thicker the better.

Pour this into a gallon container. Do the same with the rest of the beans. Be careful not to fill jar more than ⅔ full, as this mixture will separate and expand. The water will go to the bottom and the tofu "cheese" will rise to the top within 8 hours. Refrigerate.

For a firmer cheese, press in cheesecloth by hand or in a tofu press.

*Note: For a spread, mash tofu with tahini, tamari soy sauce, and finely chopped vegetables.*

---

|  |  |
|---|---|
| 2 avocadoes | 1 crushed garlic clove |
| ¼ cup sour cream | 2 medium peeled, seeded, |
| 2 tablespoons minced green | chopped tomatoes |
| onions | 1 teaspoon chopped |
| 4 teaspoons lemon juice | jalapeno peppers |
| ½ teaspoon chili powder |  |

## Latin Lover

Mash avocadoes; blend in sour cream, onions, lemon juice, chili powder, and garlic. Fold in tomatoes and add peppers.

Serve as a dip for vegetables or as stuffing for peppers or avocado shells.

**Yield: 3 cups**

*Variation: Omit tomatoes and stuff cherry tomatoes with avocado mixture.*

---

|  |  |
|---|---|
| 2 tablespoons ground | 1 teaspoon marjoram |
| sunflower seeds | 1 teaspoon tamari soy sauce |
| 6 medium minced | 1 cup ricotta cheese |
| mushrooms |  |
| sprinkling watercress or |  |
| radish sprouts |  |

## Mushroom Spread and Stuffing

Mix all ingredients but cheese in a small bowl. Add cheese in thirds, mixing thoroughly after each addition.

Use as a spread, stuffing for celery, or roll up in lettuce or Chinese cabbage leaves.

**Yield: 1 cup**

2 pounds plums, apricots,     ⅓ unpeeled lemon
          or peaches        ¼ cup honey

## Plum Butter

Puree fruit and lemon. Add honey and stir until completely dissolved.
Pour into pint or half-pint jars and freeze.

**Yield: 1 pint**

---

¾ cup diced radishes
¼ cup minced watercress
          leaves                  3 tablespoons mayonnaise

## Radish Sandwich Spread

Thoroughly mix ingredients.
Refrigerate before serving.

**Yield: 1 cup**

---

5 finely chopped celery      1 cup ground sunflower
          stalks                 seeds
4 finely chopped green       ⅓ cup ground almonds
          onions             6 tablespoons orange juice
½ cup finely chopped         4 tablespoons lemon juice
          parsley

## Santa Cruz Special

Mix ingredients thoroughly in a medium-size bowl.
Serve as a dip with fruit and vegetables or use as a tasty stuffing for avocado halves, tomatoes, and red peppers.

**Yield: 2⅔ cups**

1 tablespoon lemon juice
1 tablespoon minced onions
¼ cup crumbled blue
   cheese

1 cup sour cream
celery stalks
paprika or minced parsley
   for garnish

## Savory Celery Stuffing

Combine and thoroughly mix all ingredients but celery. Fill celery stalks with cheese mixture and chill.

Sprinkle the stuffed celery with paprika or minced parsley before serving.

**Yield: 1¼ cups**

---

2¼ cups sesame seeds
2¼ cups sunflower seeds
3 stalks celery
1 cup oil
½ cup parsley

½ cup coarsely chopped onions
3 garlic cloves
1 teaspoon tamari soy sauce
   or to taste
½ cup cider vinegar

## Seed Sandwich Spread

Process seeds in an electric blender and remove. Then process remaining ingredients in the blender and liquefy. Blend in seed mixture.

Use as a spread between 2 slices cucumber, squash, or firm tomato or as a filling for celery stalks.

**Yield: about 5 cups**

---

¼ cup grated cabbage
3 tablespoons chopped celery
3 tablespoons chopped carrots

3 tablespoons chopped
   green peppers
¼ cup mayonnaise

## Vegetable Sandwich Spread

Mix ingredients thoroughly. Refrigerate.

Can also be used as a relish or a stuffing for tomatoes.

**Yield: 1 cup**

3 large finely chopped
green peppers
1 tablespoon lemon juice
2 tablespoons olive oil

2 tablespoons mayonnaise
1 cup cottage cheese
1 minced garlic clove
⅓ cup chopped walnuts

## Walnut-Pepper Spread

Mix ingredients in a medium-size bowl until thoroughly blended. Refrigerate until ready to serve.

**Yield: about 4 cups**

---

½ cup butter
¾ cup finely ground
watercress or parsley
½ tablespoon lemon juice
(optional)

¼ cup chopped walnuts
¼ cup grated cheese
1 tablespoon minced onions

## Watercress or Parsley Butter Sandwich Spread

Cream butter. Add remaining ingredients. Stir until well blended. Use as a sandwich spread. Spreads easier at room temperature.

**Yield: 1 cup**

# Sweet Snacks

# Sweet Snacks

2¼ cups almond butter or paste
½ cup shredded coconut
¼ cup honey

¼ cup vanilla oil (not extract; there's a great difference in flavor)

## Almond Vanilla Candy

Combine ingredients and roll into 1-inch round balls. Refrigerate before serving.

**Yield: 24   1-inch balls**

*Note: For a nice change, roll balls in sesame seeds or carob powder.*

---

½ pound dried apricots
½ pound pitted dates

¼ cup honey
1½ cups shredded coconut

## Apricot Chews

Soak apricots in warm water to cover for 30 minutes. Drain well.

Finely chop fruits and gradually blend honey into mixture. Add coconut and mix thoroughly.

Press mixture into a lightly oiled 9-inch square pan. Place in the refrigerator about 1 hour to chill.

Remove from refrigerator and cut into bars or squares and serve.

**Yield: about 1¼ pounds**

---

2 cups whole wheat flour
¼ cup honey
1 cup mashed bananas

2 eggs
pure vanilla extract

## Banana Bread

Mix ingredients in a large bowl. Turn mixture onto a board and knead in enough flour until dough can be handled without being sticky.

Wrap dough in wax paper and chill in the refrigerator overnight or until roll is firm.

Slice thinly.

**Yield: 1   3 × 8-inch roll**

3 halved crosswise bananas    ½ cup honey
(with a wooden stick in    ¼ cup chopped peanuts
     the cut end)

## Banana Split Stick

Dip bananas in honey until coated, then roll in peanuts. Place on a cookie sheet and freeze until solid.

Place in a plastic container in the freezer for storage.

**Yield: 6 sticks**

---

1½ cups whole wheat flour    ⅔ cup crushed blueberries
1 cup filbert nut flour    ¼ cup honey
½ teaspoon kelp

## Blueberry Bread

Combine wheat flour with nut flour, add kelp. Stir in berries and honey. Mix with fingers, form into ball.

Dust rolling surface and rolling pin with flour. Roll out, dusting top of dough lightly as needed to keep from sticking to pin. Roll to ¼-inch thick. Cut into rectangles.

Put in dryer until completely dry.

**Yield: 18   2-inch squares**

---

⅔ cup coconut oil    1 teaspoon pure vanilla
⅓ cup honey      extract
¾ cup carob powder    ¼ cup cashews
¼ cup heavy cream    ¾ cup other chopped nuts
1 teaspoon oil

## Carob Fudge

Process all ingredients but nuts in an electric blender. Fold in nuts.

Pour or press into an oiled, 8-inch square pan and place in the refrigerator. When firm, cut into squares. Keep refrigerated.

**Yield: about 16 squares**

½ cup oat flour
¼ cup wheat germ
½ cup triticale flour
¾ cup ground almonds
½ cup finely grated carrots

1 tablespoon lemon juice
1 slightly beaten egg
2 tablespoons pineapple
 juice
¾ cup chopped raisins

## Carrot and Almond Bars

Combine ingredients in a bowl. Mix well. Spread onto a flat 8-inch square cake pan. Set in the sun to dry.

*Yield: 24 bars*

1 cup ground coconut
2 cups almond meal
2 cups ground dried
 pineapple

honey to taste
½ cup dried coconut

## Coconut and Pineapple Goody

Mix ground coconut, almond meal, and pineapple. Add honey. Roll out flat, but thick.

Cut into 2-inch squares and roll in dried coconut. Refrigerate to harden.

*Yield: 16 squares*

12 pitted dates   12 walnut halves
¼ cup peanut butter

## Dates Supreme

Slice date open, spread with peanut butter, place walnut on it, and close with the other half of the date.

*Yield: 12 dates*

¾ cup dried figs
¾ cup shredded coconut
½ cup ground nuts
1 teaspoon grated lemon rind

1 teaspoon lemon juice
finely shredded coconut for garnish

## Fig-Coconut Balls

Soak figs. With scissors, clip off stems and grind or chop fine.

Combine all ingredients but the last and work to a paste. Add more lemon juice if necessary.

Shape mixture into little balls about ¾ inch in diameter and roll in coconut.

**Yield: 12 balls**

---

20 dried figs
½ cup raisins
1 cup pecans

6 tablespoons peanut butter
crushed peanuts (optional)

## Fig Gems

With medium screen on food grinder, grind figs, raisins, and nuts. Stir together with peanut butter until soft enough to make fruit pliable. With your hands, make balls the size of small walnuts.

Can be rolled in crushed peanuts if desired.

**Yield: 20 balls**

---

1 cantaloupe
3 cups seedless green grapes
1½ chunked pineapples
3 cups strawberries
1½ cups plain yogurt
4½ tablespoons peanut butter
2 cups sour cream, divided

¾ teaspoon cinnamon
4 teaspoons honey, divided
¼ teaspoon pure vanilla extract
¼ teaspoon almond extract
1½ tablespoons finely ground walnuts

## Fresh Fruit Dips

Scoop cantaloupe into balls. Chill all fruit.

In a small bowl, mix yogurt and peanut butter.

In another small bowl, mix 1 cup sour cream, cinnamon, 2 teaspoons honey, and vanilla.

In a third small bowl, mix 1 cup sour cream, 2 teaspoons honey, almond extract, and walnuts.

Drain melon balls and pineapple chunks. Arrange all fruit around bowls of dips on a large platter. Serve immediately using food picks for dipping.

*Yield: 6 servings*

## Frozen Flower Fancy

Use only edible varieties of flowers in season. Immerse them face-down in a wide glass bowl that contains about 1 inch of water. Place bowl in the freezer.

After water is frozen, turn it out onto a bed of crushed ice and arrange fruit or vegetables around this. Flowers hold their color well with this method.

Lemon slices, flowers, or mint sprigs may also be frozen in ice cubes to enhance cold drinks.

any chunked fruits                    orange juice

## Fruit Pops

Place fruit in paper cups. Cover with orange juice and freeze partially.

Insert wooden sticks or spoons and freeze firm.

Peel off paper to serve.

½ cup honey
½ cup chopped almonds
½ cup chopped walnuts

½ cup diced orange peel
½ pound pitted dates

## Greek Dates

Mix honey, nuts, and orange peel. Stuff dates with mixture.
To preserve freshness, wrap dates individually in plastic wrap.

**Yield: about 14 stuffed dates**

---

¾ cup soaked grain (see
Index)
½ cup apple juice

3 tablespoons golden raisins
1 tablespoon honey
1 cup soybean grits

## Grit and Grain
## Silver Dollar Snacks

Process grain, apple juice, raisins, and honey in an electric blender
at medium speed 30-45 seconds.

Transfer mixture to a bowl and stir in grits until well mixed. Let
stand at room temperature 15 minutes.

Using your hands, roll spoonfuls of mixture into small balls about 1
inch in diameter. Flatten each ball so that it is the size of a silver dollar.

Place on a cake rack to dry at room temperature 24 hours.

**Yield: about 30 snacks**

*Note: To store, place dried snacks in a covered container in the refrigerator,
where they will keep for several days.*

3 cups whole wheat flour          1 cup lemon juice
½ cup honey          ½ cup thick cream

# Lemon Bread

Pour flour into a large bowl. Combine honey, lemon juice, and cream in a separate bowl, then add to flour. Mix and knead until mixture is a fine dough.

Roll dough on floured board and cut into cookies, or roll dough into a roll. Wrap in wax paper and refrigerate until firm.

Slice when firm.

**Yield: 16 cookies or 1   3×8-inch roll**

---

1 cup peanuts
1 cup rolled oats          2 cups raisins

# No-Bake Cookie

Pass peanuts through a food grinder. Mix with oats and put through a second time. Add raisins and grind once more.

Press into a square 8-inch baking dish. Cover and refrigerate before slicing into 2-inch squares.

**Yield: 16 squares**

*Note: This will keep 1-2 weeks if refrigerated.*

*Variation: Instead of pressing mixture into a pan, shape it into balls, then roll in shredded coconut or chopped peanuts. Cover and refrigerate.*

¾ cup soaked, chopped pitted prunes
1 cup blended pineapple

1 mashed banana
1 cup plain yogurt
½ teaspoon pure vanilla

## Prune Pops

Combine ingredients and spoon into 6  3-ounce paper cups. Freeze partially, insert wooden sticks or spoons, and freeze firm. Peel off paper to eat.

**Yield: 6 pops**

---

5 tablespoons honey
4 teaspoons safflower or peanut oil
⅓ cup shredded coconut
½ cup wheat germ

⅓ cup cashew or peanut pieces
¼ cup seedless raisins
½ teaspoon pure vanilla extract
⅓ cup rye flour

## Sons of Cockashew

Mix ingredients with hands and shape into 1-inch balls. May be kept in refrigerator or freezer if using at a later date.

**Yield: 6-8  1-inch balls**

---

1 cup wheat sprouts
1 cup pecans, walnuts, or sunflower seeds

1 cup raisins
1 tablespoon honey
shredded coconut

## Sprout Confections

Chop sprouts, nuts, and raisins (use a food chopper, food grinder, or wooden chopping bowl). Add honey and mix well.

Form into 1-inch balls and roll in coconut.

**Yield: 12-15  1-inch balls**

1 cup wheat sprouts  ½ cup plus 1 tablespoon
1 cup ground walnuts      cream cheese
1 cup raisins

## Sprouted Wheat and Cheese Balls

Mix well. Shape into 1-inch balls.
Keep refrigerated.

**Yield: 36 balls**

---

1 cup chopped dates  2 cups mashed bananas
1 cup chopped figs   4 cups peanut flour
1 cup finely chopped
        walnuts

## Sunbaked Fruit Bread

Combine ingredients and knead well.
Shape into wafers and bake 1 hour in the sun. Then turn and bake awhile longer. Store refrigerated in a covered dish.

**Yield: 36   2-inch squares**

---

1 cup raw milk   ⅛ cup carob powder or to taste

## Triple-Decker Fudgy-Sicles

Mix ingredients and pour into ice pop molds or paper cups with spoons or sticks in them.
Freeze. Carob settles to the bottom, making "fudge," cream rises to the top and tastes like ice cream, and the middle is like a carob-flavored ice pop.

**Yield: 2   4-ounce fudgy-sicles**

*Note: For a nice change, finely chopped fruit could be added, such as pineapple or coconut.*

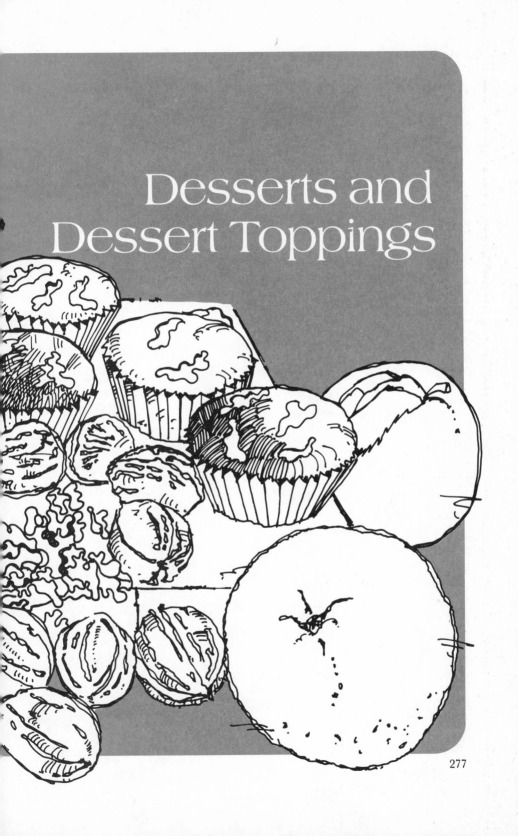

# Desserts and Dessert Toppings

# Desserts and Dessert Toppings

# I. Desserts

6 unpeeled, cored,    ½ cup chopped dates
shredded apples    1½ cups plain yogurt
1 tablespoon lemon juice    chopped nuts (optional)

## Apple Delight

In a mixing bowl, combine apples, lemon juice, and dates.
Fold in yogurt and garnish with nuts if desired.

**Yield: 6 servings**

---

1 cup ground walnuts    1½ cups chopped walnuts
¼ cup currants    3 cups grated apples,
¼ cup tahini     sprinkled with ½ juiced lemon
¼ cup honey    2 tablespoons honey
½ teaspoon cinnamon    ¾ cup raisins
½ cup ground almonds    1 teaspoon cinnamon

## Apple Pie

Mix first 6 ingredients. Set aside ½ cup for topping. Press remaining
mix into 9-inch pie plate. Chill.

Mix remaining ingredients and pour into bottom crust. Top with
remaining ½ cup reserved crust.

**Yield: 1   9-inch pie**

---

5 pureed apples    1 teaspoon grated lemon
⅛ cup honey     rind
4 tablespoons lemon juice    1½ cups milk

## Apple Sherbet

Combine ingredients and mix well.

Pour into ice tray and freeze at coldest temperature until almost
firm; turn into a chilled bowl and beat until smooth.

Return to ice tray and refreeze.

**Yield: 6 servings**

| 1 envelope (1 tablespoon) | 1 tablespoon honey |
| unflavored gelatin | 2 cored, chopped apples |
| ¼ cup cold water | 1 Piecrust (see Index) |
| 2 mashed avocadoes | 1 cup plain yogurt |
| 2 tablespoons lemon juice | |

## Avocado-Apple Pie Filling

Sprinkle gelatin over the cold water in a small heat-resistant cup and let stand 5 minutes to soften. Place in a pan of hot (140°F.) water, stirring until gelatin is dissolved.

Mash avocadoes with lemon juice and honey. Add dissolved gelatin to mixture and beat with a rotary mixer until smooth.

Chill until mixture forms a mound when dropped from a spoon. Chop apples directly into mixture to prevent them from discoloring. Stir until mixed.

Mound mixture into piecrust and chill until set.

Slice into 6 portions and top each with a dollop of yogurt.

**Yield: 6 servings**

---

| 3 diced avocadoes | 3 peeled, quartered apples |
| 1 cup pineapple chunks | nuts for garnish |
| 2 juiced lemons | |

## Avocado Chiller

Process ingredients in an electric blender until smooth. Chill. Garnish with nuts and serve immediately.

**Yield: 6 cups**

---

| 4 cups cold carrot juice | 3 chilled halved avocadoes |
| 2 stiffly beaten egg whites | ½ cup shredded coconut |

## Avocado Stuffed with Carrot Ice

Set refrigerator temperature control at highest point for fast freezing. Chill 2 empty ice trays. When cold, pour 2 cups carrot juice into each tray and freeze until almost firm, about 45 minutes–1 hour, stirring occasionally.

Turn both trays of juice into a large bowl; break up any lumps and beat with a rotary or electric mixer until smooth. The juice should be slushy, but not melted. Fold in egg whites and return mixture to ice trays.

Cover with foil to prevent ice crystals from forming and freeze until firm.

Just before serving, prepare avocadoes. Using an ice cream dipper, place a portion of carrot ice in each avocado half and sprinkle with coconut. Serve immediately.

**Yield: 6 servings**

*Note: Carrot Ice should be used the same day it is made; otherwise it will set too firmly.*

---

| | |
|---|---|
| 1½ cups finely chopped peanuts | 1 cup cottage cheese (blended) or plain yogurt |
| 4 tablespoons softened butter | 1 tablespoon honey |
| 3 mashed bananas | ¼ teaspoon pure vanilla extract |

## Banana Pie

Chop peanuts in an electric blender. Reserve 2 tablespoons.

In a 9-inch pie plate, mix remaining chopped nuts and butter thoroughly. Press nut mixture evenly on bottom and sides of pie plate to form crust. Chill at least 1 hour.

Mix bananas, cottage cheese, honey, and vanilla and use mixture to fill piecrust.

Sprinkle 2 tablespoons nuts on pie and freeze at least 3 hours.

Remove pie from freezer to refrigerator 3-4 hours before serving.

**Yield: 1   9-inch pie**

*Note: If you dip bottom of pie plate in warm water about 1 minute before serving, pie will be easier to remove from plate.*

| | |
|---|---|
| chicory | ½ cup plain yogurt |
| 3 peeled, halved avocadoes | 2 pounds seedless green |
| ½ juiced lemon | grapes |
| 6 ounces room temperature | 1 cup pine nuts (pignoli) |
| cream cheese | Strawberry Dressing (see Index) |

# Bunch of Grapes

Cover each plate with a bed of chicory.

Sprinkle cut sides of avocadoes with lemon juice. Place an avocado, cutside down, on each chicory bed.

Mix cream cheese and yogurt and spread on each avocado.

Cut grapes in half and arrange them cutside down on the covered avocado so that they resemble a bunch of grapes. Slip a pine nut underneath each grape half.

Serve cold with dressing.

**Yield: 6 servings**

---

| | |
|---|---|
| ¼ cup warm water | 1 cup ricotta cheese |
| 1 envelope (1 tablespoon) | ½ cup heavy cream |
| unflavored gelatin | ⅛ teaspoon pure vanilla or |
| ¼ cup honey | almond extract |
| 1 cup cottage cheese | fruit for garnish |

# Coeur a la Creme

Oil a smooth 1-quart mold.

Pour water into an electric blender, sprinkle gelatin on top. Cover and process at low speed until gelatin is dissolved, about 1 minute. Remove cover while processing and add honey. Turn control to high speed, gradually add cottage and ricotta cheese and continue processing until smooth. Remove feeder cap and add cream and flavoring. Process only until mixture is well blended.

Pour into prepared mold and chill until firm.

To serve, unmold on a serving dish and garnish with fruit.

**Yield: 6-8 servings**

3 1-inch-sliced slightly    ½ cup apple juice, if
    frozen bananas               needed, to blend
    4 pitted dates    1 chilled Piecrust (see
1 teaspoon cinnamon            Index)

## Creamy Banana-Date Pie

Combine ingredients in an electric blender and process until creamy.

Pour into piecrust.

*Yield: 1   9-inch pie*

---

1 envelope (1 tablespoon)    1½ teaspoon pure vanilla
    unflavored gelatin       2 tablespoons honey
    ¼ cup cold water         ¾ tablespoon sesame seeds
    3 cups plain yogurt      ¾ teaspoon sunflower seeds
            1 egg    pinch nutmeg or cinnamon

## C's Crumbly Custard

Sprinkle gelatin over the cold water in a small heat-resistant cup and let stand 5 minutes to soften. Place in a pan of hot (140°F.) water, stirring until gelatin is dissolved.

Process yogurt, egg, vanilla, and honey in an electric blender. Add gelatin while blender is whirling.

Pour into a bowl and sprinkle with topping of seeds and spice. Cover and refrigerate until set.

*Yield: 6 servings*

---

2 sticks agar-agar    ½ pint blueberries
2 cups cold water    ½ pint sliced strawberries
1 quart apple juice    3 thinly sliced peaches
    ½ cup honey    ¼ cup tahini

## Fresh Fruit Dessert

Soak agar-agar in water 15 minutes. Then boil it slowly another 15 minutes.

[continued on next page]

Add juice and honey and let sit until cool.
Add fruit and tahini and stir.
Pour into a serving bowl and refrigerate until thickened.

*Yield: 6–8 servings*

---

2 sticks agar-agar  1 teaspoon pure vanilla extract
1 cup water   1 pint plain yogurt
½ cup honey   1 Piecrust (see Index)
1½ quarts orange juice  ¼ cup ground nuts
1 grated orange rind  mint sprigs

## Fresh Orange Pie

Soak agar-agar in water 15 minutes. Then boil it slowly another 15 minutes. Remove from heat.

Add honey, juice, rind, and vanilla. Stir. Put aside to cool.

With wire whisk gently fold in yogurt. Put in pie shell and sprinkle with nuts.

Refrigerate until somewhat firm.

Serve encircled with mint sprigs.

*Yield: 1   9-inch pie*

---

4 cups plain yogurt  2 cups chopped sweet cherries
1 tablespoon honey  2 diced bananas
4 tablespoons lemon juice  ½ cup chopped nuts (such
¼ teaspoon grated lemon   as almonds, pecans, or
rind   cashews)

## Frozen Fruit Yogurt

Fold ingredients together and spoon into muffin papers, which have been placed in muffin tins.

Freeze until firm.

Set pans at room temperature a few minutes before serving. Use a table knife to loosen and remove yogurt from papers.

*Yield: 24 muffin-size yogurts*

| | |
|---|---|
| 1 cup currants | 1 tablespoon orange rind |
| 1 cup seedless raisins | 2 cups chopped pecans |
| 2¼ cups (1 pound) pitted dates | 1 cup chopped almonds |
| | 2 cups grated coconut |
| 1½ cups (1 pound) dried apricots | 1 teaspoon cinnamon |
| | 3 tablespoons lemon juice |
| 1 large peeled, chopped orange | ¼-⅓ cup honey |
| | ⅓ cup sesame seeds |

## Fruit Squares

Soak currants, raisins, dates, and apricots in warm water 15 minutes. Drain well. Add orange pieces. Chop all fruit finely.

Mix and add orange rind, nuts, coconut, cinnamon, and lemon juice. Blend honey into mixture.

Pack mixture into a 12×16-inch jelly-roll pan. Cover with sesame seeds and refrigerate.

Chill well and cut into squares before serving.

**Yield: 48   2-inch squares**

| | |
|---|---|
| 1 cup almonds | |
| 1 cup apple juice | |
| 2 cups strawberries, peaches, or other fruit | 1 banana |
| | 2 tablespoons oil |

## Fruity Nut Cream

Process ingredients in an electric blender.

Pour mixture into a container and place in the freezer 1-2 hours. Do not allow it to freeze solid.

**Yield: 6   ½-cup servings**

6 peeled, sectioned red   1 cup raisins or Grecian figs
grapefruit   1 cup chopped walnuts or
3 sliced bananas   almonds

# Grapefruit Cup

Squeeze juice and pulp of grapefruit into a medium-size bowl. Add bananas, raisins, and nuts. Mix well.
Serve chilled.

**Yield: 6 servings**

---

¾ cup grape juice   ½ cup honey
1 juiced lemon   1 pint heavy cream

# Grape Ice Cream

Mix grape juice, lemon juice, and honey.
Whip cream and gradually add honey-juice mixture, beating well after each addition.
Freeze until firm.

**Yield: 6 servings**

---

1 medium honeydew melon   2 tablespoons honey
6 large grape leaves   whole almonds for garnish
2 cups pitted black cherries   1 lime, cut into 6 pieces

# Honeydew Supreme

Slice honeydew into 1-inch-thick rings. Cut off rind. Place grape leaf on plates.

In a small bowl, mix cherries and honey. Place ¼ cup of mixture in the center of each honeydew slice.

Place an almond on each mound of cherries. Serve chilled with a slice of lime.

**Yield: 6 servings**

2 cups dry cottage cheese
2 cups creamed cottage
    cheese
8 teaspoons honey

1 teaspoon pure vanilla
    extract
2 cups berries

## Instant Fruited Cheese Parfait

Process cottage cheese, honey, and vanilla in an electric blender until smooth.

Layer mixture into clear parfait glasses, alternating with berries. End with a dollop of the cheese mixture and top with a berry.

**Yield: 6 servings**

1 envelope (1 tablespoon)
    plus 1 teaspoon gelatin
3 tablespoons honey
¾ cup warm water
1¾ cups orange juice
1½ tablespoons lemon juice

3 segmented oranges
1½ sliced bananas
6 tablespoons shredded
    coconut
mayonnaise or whipped
    cream to garnish

## Jellied Ambrosia

Mix gelatin and honey. Add warm water. Stir until completely dissolved. Add orange and lemon juice. Chill until partially set.

Cut orange segments in pieces, reserving a few whole segments for garnish. Fold orange pieces, sliced bananas, and coconut into gelatin.

Pour into a 4½-cup mold. Chill until firm.

Unmold and garnish with orange segments. Serve with mayonnaise or whipped cream.

**Yield: 6   ½-cup servings**

3 halved avocadoes  
¾ cup sour cream or  
  blended cottage cheese  
4 tablespoons honey

¼ teaspoon pure vanilla  
  extract  
seedless grapes for garnish

## Malaysian Avocado Dessert

Scoop avocado pulp from shells leaving shells intact.

Mash avocado until smooth. Mix in sour cream and honey, blending well. Stir in vanilla and return mixture to shells. Chill well.

Before serving, garnish each avocado half with a grape.

***Yield: 6 servings***

---

3 tablespoons grated lemon  
  peel  
1 tablespoon honey  
½ cup lime juice

2 cups honeydew balls  
2 cups cantaloupe balls  
mint leaves for garnish

## Melons with Lime

Mix lemon peel, honey, and lime juice.

Place melon balls in a glass or ceramic bowl, add mixture, and refrigerate 2 hours.

Garnish with mint leaves before serving.

***Yield: 6 servings***

---

½ cup dried apricots  
½ cup dried apples  
¼ cup raisins  
¼ cup peanut butter

1 tablespoon honey  
½ cup whipping cream  
2 teaspoons honey

## Nutty Fruit Tarts

With scissors, cut apricots into small pieces. Cover with water and soak 30 minutes.

With scissors, cut apples into small pieces. In a small bowl, mix together apples and raisins. Add peanut butter and mix well.

Drain apricots, squeezing out excess water. Mix apricots with honey.

Lightly butter or oil bottoms and sides of a 6-cup muffin tin. Place apricots in cups, pressing lightly.

Then press apple mixture lightly on apricots. Refrigerate at least 1 hour.

In a small bowl, beat cream until stiff. Fold in honey.

Loosen tarts by running the blade of a knife around sides of cups. Turn tarts out and top each with a dollop of whipped cream.

*Yield: 6 tarts*

---

1 cup chilled whipping cream

1 tablespoon grated orange rind

⅓ cup orange juice

¼ cup honey

## Orange Cream Sherbet

Process ingredients in an electric blender until thick.

Pour into 1-quart freezer container and freeze overnight or until firm.

*Yield: about 1 quart*

---

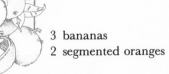
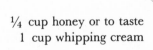

¼ cup honey or to taste

1 cup whipping cream

3 bananas

2 segmented oranges

## Orange Fluff

Add honey to cream and whip stiff.

Mash bananas to a pulp. Add to cream mixture. Fold in oranges. Serve immediately in parfait glasses.

*Yield: 6 servings*

1 cup whipping cream   ¼ cup chopped pecans or
6 persimmons   other nuts (optional)

# Persimmon Puff

Whip cream until stiff. Refrigerate. Cap persimmons and remove seeds.

Process in an electric blender. Spoon desired amount into individual serving dishes.

Top with whipped cream. If desired, sprinkle with chopped nuts.

**Yield: 6   ½-cup servings**

---

½ cup ground almonds   ¼ cup peanut butter
½ cup ground walnuts   ¼ cup honey
¼ cup ground sunflower seeds   pinch coriander

# Piecrust

Mix ingredients. Press into a 9-inch pie plate.
Chill thoroughly before filling.

**Yield: 1   9-inch piecrust**

---

2½ cups pineapple juice   1 cup cashews
2 tablespoons heavy cream   ½ cup oil
½ cup clover honey

# Pineapple Sherbet

Process ingredients in an electric blender, adding oil last. Pour into an ice tray and freeze.

Remove from tray and process in blender again.

Return to ice tray and refreeze.

**Yield: 6 servings**

1 cup cottage cheese
½ cup plain yogurt
2 tablespoons honey
¼ teaspoon pure vanilla extract

½ cup blended pineapple
1 Piecrust (see Index)
2 tablespoons chopped nuts

## Pineapple-Yogurt Cheese Pie

Mix cheese, yogurt, honey, and vanilla. Then add pineapple and mix well.

Pour into piecrust. Chill well, topping with chopped nuts.

*Yield: 1    9-inch pie*

---

1 cup (2 pomegranates)
pomegranate seeds

1 cup chopped filberts
2 tablespoons honey

## Pomegranate Delight

Combine ingredients.

Serve small portions in clear dessert glasses.

*Yield: 4    ½-cup servings*

---

¾ cup chopped prunes
2 tablespoons honey

2 unbeaten egg whites
1 teaspoon lemon juice

## Prune Froth Parfait

Soak prunes in water to cover 3 hours or until softened. Drain.

Beat ingredients at high speed in an electric mixer 5 minutes until froth holds its shape.

Spoon into serving dishes; chill.

*Yield: 6 servings*

1 stick agar-agar
2 cups water
¾ cup honey
1 pint mashed raspberries
or wine berries

¼ teaspoon almond extract
1 pint plain yogurt
1 Wheat and Coconut
Piecrust (see Index)

## Raspberry-Yogurt Pie

Soak agar-agar in water 15 minutes. Then boil it slowly another 15 minutes.

Add honey, berries, and almond extract, and stir well. Allow to set until semifirm.

With wire whisk gently fold in yogurt. Gently spoon into piecrust. Refrigerate until well chilled.

**Yield: 1   8-inch pie**

2 cups bulgur (see Index)
½ cup raisins
1 cup crushed pineapple
½ cup pineapple juice

½ teaspoon cinnamon
½ teaspoon rosemary
plain yogurt (optional)

## Rosemary-Raisin Bulgur

In a large bowl, mix bulgur and raisins. Add warm water to about 1 inch above bulgur. Allow to soak 1½ hours.

Press out excess water by placing bulgur in a strainer and pushing gently with the back of a large spoon.

Add remaining ingredients and chill well before serving in soup bowls.

Top with plain yogurt if desired.

**Yield: 6   1-cup servings**

2 tablespoons honey
1 teaspoon lemon juice
½ pound halved, seeded
  white grapes
½ pound halved, seeded
  red grapes
1 tablespoon slivered
  almonds

## Syruped Grapes

Warm honey with lemon juice. Place grapes in a bowl, then add honey mixture.

Marinate 2 hours at room temperature, then refrigerate.

Serve in individual bowls and decorate with almonds.

**Yield: 4-6 servings**

---

¾ cup soaked wheat (see
  Index)
¼ cup shredded coconut
¼ cup softened butter

## Wheat and Coconut Piecrust

Combine ingredients in a mixing bowl.

Transfer mixture to a 7½- or 8-inch pie plate. Using a spatula, spread mixture evenly over the bottom and sides of the plate.

Place in the refrigerator to chill.

**Yield: 1   7½- or 8-inch piecrust**

---

2 cubed bananas
2 cubed pears
2 cubed apples
12 chopped pitted dates
4 juiced tangerines
½ cup ground walnuts

## Winter Fruits

Toss fruits with juice.

Refrigerate 1 hour.

Sprinkle with walnuts before serving.

**Yield: 6 servings**

2 tablespoons honey or to taste
1 tablespoon lemon juice
2 sectioned oranges
1 unpeeled, diced red apple

1 sliced banana
1 unpeeled, diced pear
½ cup shredded coconut
1 cup plain yogurt

## Yogurt Ambrosia

Combine honey and lemon juice in a mixing bowl, then add fruits. Toss gently until coated. Chill.

Just before serving, add yogurt, then toss. Serve immediately.

*Yield: 6 servings*

# II. Dessert Toppings

1 cup whipping cream
6 tablespoons carob powder
2 teaspoons honey

½ teaspoon pure vanilla extract

## Carob Cream Topping

Using a chilled mixer bowl, whip cream about ½ minute until it bubbles. Quickly add carob, honey, and vanilla. Beat until cream fluffs into peaks.

Refrigerate.

Serve as topping for fruit.

*Yield: 1½ cups*

3 tablespoons carob powder
½ cup plain yogurt
½ cup honey

1 teaspoon pure vanilla extract
1 tablespoon butter

## Carob Yogurt Topping

Process ingredients in an electric blender.

Spoon over fruit or eat separately as a dessert.

*Yield: 1½ cups*

1 cup dark sweet cherries
½ cup ground almonds          ¼ teaspoon lemon juice

## Cherry Topping

Process ingredients in an electric blender until well blended.
Serve as a topping for fruit or yogurt or eat separately as a dessert.

**Yield: 1 cup**

---

4 tablespoons butter    2 ounces heavy cream
½ cup honey

## Honey Cream Topping

Process butter and honey in an electric blender or food processor.
Add cream gradually and keep blending until soft and foamy.
Use as topping for fruit.

**Yield: about ⅔ cup**

---

2 cups plain yogurt    2 tablespoons lemon juice
¼ cup honey    ½ teaspoon pure vanilla
2 teaspoons grated lemon rind    extract

## Honey 'n' Yogurt Topping

In small bowl or an electric blender, combine and mix together all
ingredients.
Serve over fruit or separately as a dessert.

**Yield: 2 cups**

2 cups chunked pineapple   sunflower seeds
ground almonds

# Pineapple Topping

Process pineapple in an electric blender until smooth.
In a bowl, add nuts and seeds until consistency is thick and jamlike.
Keep refrigerated.
Use as topping for yogurt or fruit or serve separately as a dessert.

**Yield: 2 cups**

# Metric Conversion

## Mass (weight)

| | | |
|---|---|---|
| 1 ounce | 28 | grams |
| 1 pound | 454 | grams |

## Volume

| | | |
|---|---|---|
| 1 teaspoon | 5 | milliliters |
| 1 tablespoon | 15 | milliliters |
| 1 ounce | 30 | milliliters |
| 1 cup | 0.24 liter | |
| 1 pint | 0.47 liter | |
| 1 quart | 0.95 liter | |
| 1 gallon | 3.8 | liters |

# Index

# Q

Quick Bean Dish, 240
Quick Summer Beans, 184

# R

Radishes
  Cashew Cheese Dressing, 163
  Cottage Cheese Loaf, 180
  Cucumbers and Radishes in Sour
    Cream, 235
  Jardiniere Platter, 198
  Radish Cocktail, 120
  Radish Sandwich Spread, 260
  Red and Green Vegetables on
    Grain Beds, 217
Raisins
  A.M. Salad with Yogurt, 101
  Applacado Salad, 149
  Breakfast Salad, 103
  Cabbage Waldorf Salad, 149
  Cottage-Applesauce Mold, 204
  Curried Waldorf Salad, 150
  Energy Glow Breakfast, 104
  Fig Gems, 270
  Fruit Soup, 140
  Fruit Squares, 285
  Grapefruit Cup, 286
  Israeli Carrot Salad, 151
  No-Bake Cookie, 273
  Peanut and Banana Soup, 141
  Pear Crunch Salad, 152
  Rosemary-Raisin Bulgur, 292
  Sprouted Wheat and Cheese Balls,
    275
  Sunshine Special, 154
  Tropical Oats, 107
  Yogurt-Vegetable Soup, 144
Raspberries
  Raspberry-Yogurt Pie, 292
  Summer Refresher, 120

Raw, definition of, viii
Raw Creamed Soup, 142
Raw Fish with Dipping Sauce,
  192–93
Raw Spinach with Mushrooms, 158
Raw Vegetable Loaf, 199
Red and Green Vegetables on Grain
  Beds, 217
Red Cabbage Slaw, 156
Red Cottage Cheese, 185
Red snapper
  Marinated Fish Tahitian Style,
    192
Relishes. See Pickles and Relishes
Rhubarb-Apple Juice, 120
Ricotta, 58
  Artichokes in Cream, 233
  Coeur a la Creme, 282
  Confetti Cheese Mold, 203
  Mushroom Spread and Stuffing,
    259
  Ricotta Dressing, 154
  Romaine and Fennel Salad, 158
  Ruby Sandwich Filling, 255
  Rye-Ricotta Sandwich Filling, 256
  Spinach and Ricotta Balls, 132
  Stuffed Celery Wheels, 187
  Stuffed Endive, 189
Roadside stands, as food source, 45
Romaine and Fennel Salad, 158
Root cellars, for food storage, 53–54
Roquefort cheese
  Pear and Roquefort Salad, 153
  Pecan-Roquefort Hors d'Oeuvres,
    130
  Roquefort Apples, 153
  Sharp Roquefort Salad Dressing,
    167
Rosemary-Raisin Bulgur, 292
Ruby Sandwich Filling, 255
Rutabaga
  Winter Slaw, 157